WILLIAMS-SONOMA

Vegetarian for All Seasons

GENERAL EDITOR
Chuck Williams

RECIPES
Pamela Sheldon Johns

PHOTOGRAPHY
Richard Eskite

Oxmoor House®

Oxmoor House

OXMOOR HOUSE INC.
Oxmoor House books are distributed by
Sunset Books
80 Willow Road, Menlo Park, CA 94025
Phone: (650) 321-3600 Fax: (650) 324-1532

Vice President/General Manager: Rich Smeby
Director of Special Sales: Gary Wright
Oxmoor House and Sunset Books are divisions of
Southern Progress Corporation

WILLIAMS-SONOMA
Founder and Vice-Chairman: Chuck Williams
Book Buyer: Cecilia Michaelis

WELDON OWEN INC.
Chief Executive Officer: John Owen
President: Terry Newell
Chief Operating Officer: Larry Partington
Vice President, International Sales: Stuart Laurence
Associate Publisher: Lisa Atwood
Senior Editor: Hannah Rahill
Consulting Editor: Norman Kolpas
Copy Editor: Sharon Silva
Design: Kari Perin, Perin+Perin
Production Director: Stephanie Sherman
Production Manager: Jen Dalton
Production Editor: Sarah Lemas
Co-editions Director: Derek Barton
Food Stylist: George Dolese
Prop Stylist: Sara Slavin
Photo Production Coordinator: Juliann Harvey
Photo Assistants: Lara Hata, Jonathan Miller,
  Kevin Hossler
Food Styling Assistant: Jill Sorensen
Glossary Illustrations: Alice Harth

A NOTE ON WEIGHTS AND MEASURES
All recipes include customary U.S. and metric
measurements. Metric conversions are based on a
standard developed for these books and have been
rounded off. Actual weights may vary.

The Williams-Sonoma Lifestyles Series
conceived and produced by Weldon Owen Inc.
814 Montgomery Street, San Francisco, CA 94133

In collaboration with Williams-Sonoma
3250 Van Ness Avenue, San Francisco, CA 94109

Separations by Colourscan Overseas Co. Pte. Ltd.
Printed in Singapore by Tien Wah Press (Pte.) Ltd.

A WELDON OWEN PRODUCTION
Copyright © 1998 Weldon Owen Inc.
All rights reserved, including the right of reproduc-
tion in whole or in part in any form.

First printed in 1998
10 9 8 7 6 5 4 3

Library of Congress
Cataloging-in-Publication Data

Johns, Pamela Sheldon 1953–
    Vegetarian for all seasons / general editor, Chuck
  Williams; recipes by Pamela Sheldon Johns;
  photography by Richard Eskite.
      p. cm. — (Williams-Sonoma lifestyles)
    Includes index
    ISBN 0-8487-2619-7
    1. Vegetarian cookery. I. Title. II. Series.
TX837.J53 1998
641.5'636—dc21   97-28552
                                            CIP

A NOTE ON NUTRITIONAL ANALYSIS
Each recipe is analyzed for significant nutrients per
serving. Not included in the analysis are ingredients
that are optional or added to taste, or are suggested
as an alternative or substitution either in the recipe
or in the recipe introduction or accompanying tip. In
recipes that yield a range of servings, the analysis is
for the middle of that range.

Contents

Welcome

I can't think of a vegetable or fruit I don't like. In fact, if you look at my dinner table on some nights, you might think I am a vegetarian from the perfect little green beans, baby squashes, or baked potato I often enjoy as a main course.

Nowadays, those of us who love good health as much as we love good food eat like vegetarians at least some of the time. The dramatic growth in high-quality local green-grocers and farmers' markets like the one pictured here makes it easier than ever to enjoy a wide variety of peak-of-season produce.

Seasonality and variety are the keys to interesting and satisfying vegetarian cooking, and you'll find those qualities in abundance in the recipes that follow. They take full advantage of fresh seasonal produce and include fresh herbs, intriguing spices, and international influences to make vegetables, grains, and beans more appealing than ever.

We've also provided advice on how to plan well-balanced vegetarian meals; how to entertain with vegetarian menus; and how to pick, choose, and prepare the best seasonal vegetables and fruits. All along, our goal has been simple: to make cooking fresh-vegetable dishes a year-round pleasure, whether you're a full-time or an occasional vegetarian.

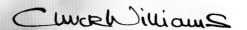

The Seasonal Vegetarian Table

With just a small garden patch, or even a windowsill, you can add abundance and diversity to your vegetarian table. Search nurseries and seed catalogs for old-fashioned heirloom tomatoes such as striped green and yellow Green Zebras, Lemon Boys or orange Valencias, planting them alongside your favorite red varieties. Most nurseries also sell herbs growing in small pots that you can tend indoors year-round.

Cooking with the Seasons

If you've ever had any doubts about the wisdom of cooking with the seasons, pick a tomato that has ripened on the vine under summer's hot sun. Rinse away any dust from its surface, then take a bite. You'll be astonished by the powerful burst of full, sweet, juicy tomato flavor, so much more intense than any hothouse-raised tomato found in most food stores.

Vegetables taste best when they've been grown as nature intended them and eaten as soon as possible after harvesting. But many people have lost sight of that simple truth in these days of scientific agriculture, international airfreight, and genetic engineering.

There are good reasons to follow the seasons when you're cooking and eating vegetarian meals. Vegetables that have enjoyed optimum growing conditions are likely to have higher nutrient levels. Their cost, meanwhile, will move in the opposite direction: Nothing drives down prices like a bumper crop!

Best of all, the taste and texture of the peak-of-season ingredients you buy or grow in your own garden will naturally be at their finest. This simple fact explains why cooking with seasonal produce can be quick, easy, and satisfying.

Bringing Variety to the Table

As the recipes in this book demonstrate, seasonal vegetarian cooking can also be highly varied. A glance at the seasonality charts on pages 10–11 will give you a good idea of the wide range of vegetables from which you can choose.

The possibilities will increase even more once you've located a good farmers' market or other provider that can offer you not only a full range of seasonal vegetables, but also a variety of choices for each particular vegetable. Seek out, in particular, the stands of growers who specialize in heirloom vegetables. These little-known strains have wonderfully rich colors, flavors, and textures.

Be sure also to have a range of fresh herbs on hand. Whether plucked from a garden, window box, or market stall, herbs will always bring extra flavor to the vegetarian table.

Planning Healthy Menus

Each of the recipes in this book includes a nutritional analysis to help you track your intake of nutrients. But this book is not meant to be a dietary guide. The responsibility for eating a balanced diet lies with you.

Following a few basic principles will help you make the most of a vegetarian lifestyle. For example, to ensure the consumption of adequate protein, rely on dishes based on dried beans and grains. Dairy products, particularly cheese and yogurt, also provide protein for some vegetarians. Bear in mind, though, that cheeses, milk, and cream can be high in fat. Enjoy dishes that feature them in moderation. Eating vegetables, fruits, nuts, and whole grains is the best way to ensure an adequate intake of dietary fiber, another important component of a healthy diet.

To add moisture and flavor to recipes without adding any fat, use vegetable stock (at right) in lieu of milk or cream. Above all, keep in mind that the best way to achieve a balanced diet is to eat a broad range of foods.

Vegetable Stock

¼ cup (2 fl oz/60 ml) extra-virgin olive oil
1 yellow onion, coarsely chopped
1 carrot, peeled and chopped
2 celery stalks, coarsely chopped
½ cup (4 fl oz/125 ml) dry white wine
4 qt (4 l) water
1 bouquet garni: 1 fresh parsley sprig, 1 fresh thyme sprig, and 1 bay leaf tied together with string
4 or 5 peppercorns

✲ In a stockpot over medium heat, warm the oil. Add the onion, carrot, and celery. Sauté until browned, 5–8 minutes. Raise the heat to high. Pour in the wine, stirring to dislodge any browned bits from the pan bottom. When the wine is almost fully evaporated, add the water, bouquet garni, and peppercorns and bring to a boil.

✲ Reduce the heat to medium and simmer gently, uncovered, for at least 45 minutes. FOR RICH STOCK, raise the heat to medium-high and boil until reduced by half, 1¼–1½ hours longer.

✲ Strain the stock into a bowl. Let cool. Store in an airtight container in the refrigerator for up to 1 week or freeze for up to 6 months.

MAKES ABOUT 3 QT (3 L) REGULAR STOCK OR 2 QT (2 L) RICH STOCK

Peak-of-Season Vegetables

SELECTING THE BEST

The seasonal lists on the right will give you an idea of what to expect when you visit your local farmers' market or other source for good seasonal produce. Bear in mind that vegetables don't watch the calendar, however, and that their availability will vary with location and weather.

There are no great secrets to picking the best produce, short of learning to use your eyes, hands, nose, and, if a friendly shopkeeper will let you, your mouth to judge the qualities of a particular bunch of asparagus, say, or a box of tomatoes. Still, the guidelines that follow offer some commonsense pointers to help you make your selections.

Shoots and Stalks
Choose straight, crisp-looking specimens with fresh, smooth cut ends. Asparagus tips and artichokes should appear tightly closed.

Leaves
Choose crisp, bright leaves with no signs of wilting. Smaller specimens generally have better flavor and texture. Younger, smaller chicories will have the best flavor and texture.

SPRING

Shoots and Stalks
Artichokes • Asparagus • Cardoons • Fennel

Leaves
Arugula • Baby Spinach • Belgian Endive • Collard Greens • Dandelion Greens • Escarole • Frisée • Kale • Lettuces • Mâche • Mustard Greens • Sorrel • Swiss Chard • Turnip Greens • Watercress

Cabbage Family
Broccoli Rabe • Cabbage

Roots and Tubers
Daikon • Jicama • New Potatoes • Radishes • Turnips • Young Ginger

Mushrooms
Buttons • Morels • Oysters • Porcini • Portobellos • Shiitakes

Peas, Beans, and Seeds
English Peas • Fava Beans • Pea Shoots • Snow Peas • Sugar Snap Peas

Bulbs
Baby Leeks • Green Garlic • Green Onions • Vidalia Onions

SUMMER

Shoots and Stalks
Cardoons

Leaves
Arugula • Romaine Lettuce • Spinach

Vegetable Fruits
Avocados • Bell Peppers • Chiles • Cucumbers • Eggplants • Okra • Summer Squashes • Tomatillos • Tomatoes • Zucchini • Zucchini Flowers

Roots and Tubers
Beets • Carrots • Ginger • Potatoes

Peas, Beans, and Seeds
Corn • English Peas • Green Beans • Haricots Verts • Shelling Beans • Wax Beans

Bulbs
Garlic • Leeks • Onions • Shallots

AUTUMN

Shoots and Stalks
Artichokes • Cardoons

Leaves
Belgian Endive • Escarole • Frisée • Radicchio • Spinach • Swiss Chard

Cabbage Family
Broccoli • Broccoli Rabe • Brussels Sprouts • Cabbage • Cauliflower

Vegetable Fruits
Bell Peppers • Eggplants • Pumpkins • Winter Squashes

Roots and Tubers
Beets • Celery Root • Parsnips • Potatoes • Radishes • Rutabagas • Sweet Potatoes • Turnips • Yams

Mushrooms
Chanterelles • Porcini • Portobellos • Shiitakes • White Mushrooms

Bulbs
Garlic • Leeks • Shallots

WINTER

Leaves
Belgian Endive • Collard Greens • Escarole • Frisée • Kale • Radicchio • Swiss Chard • Turnip Greens

Cabbage Family
Broccoli • Broccoli Rabe • Brussels Sprouts • Cabbage

Roots and Tubers
Celery Root • Jerusalem Artichokes • Jicama • Parsnips • Rutabagas • Sweet Potatoes • Turnips • Yams

Mushrooms
Chanterelles • Portobellos • Truffles • White Mushrooms

Cabbage Family
Cabbages should feel heavy for their size and be densely packed. Broccoli, broccoli rabe, and cauliflower should have compact heads and firm, crisp stalks.

Vegetable Fruits
Select heavy, firm specimens with bright, glossy skins. Ripe avocados and most tomatoes are tender to the touch. Eggplants heaviest for their size will have the fewest seeds.

Roots, Tubers, and Bulbs
Look for dry skins free from signs of spoilage. Green tops of carrots, parsnips, turnips, beets, and other roots should look fresh. Avoid potatoes with green-tinged patches or sprouting eyes.

Mushrooms
The best should feel neither dry nor moist and have a clean, fresh aroma. The caps of button mushrooms should be tightly closed.

Peas, Beans, and Seeds
Any specimens to be shelled should have plump, flexible pods that, when split open, feel moist inside. The best edible pea pods and beans will look bright and shiny and be crisp enough to snap cleanly with gentle pressure.

Spring

Little more than some simple trimming, peeling, or shelling readies springtime's signature vegetables. Remember, when working with artichokes, their flesh rapidly discolors upon exposure to air, making it necessary to dip them in water mixed with some lemon juice after cutting or trimming.

PREPARING ARTICHOKE BOTTOMS

1. Cut off the stem even with the base and cut off the top half. Trim away the tough outer layer around the base. Put in lemon water to prevent discoloring.

2. Cook as directed in the recipe. Invert and let drain until cool enough to handle. With a spoon, scrape out the choke from each base.

SHELLING AND PEELING FAVA BEANS

1. Split open the pod along the length of its seam. Run a thumb along the inside length of the pod to pop out the fava beans.

2. Boil the fava beans in water for 1 minute. Drain well. When cool enough to handle, pinch the skin at one end to split, then gently squeeze to pop out the bean.

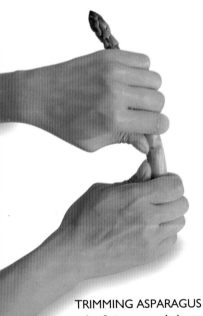

TRIMMING ASPARAGUS

A knife is not needed to trim springtime asparagus. Just grasp the stalk near its base with one hand. With the other hand, grasp and bend the cut end. It will naturally snap off at the point where the stalk becomes tender.

Summer

Summer's popular tomatoes and peppers (capsicums) have shiny skins that are easily removed. When you work with chiles, remember that their volatile oils can cause burning. Take care not to touch your eyes or other sensitive areas, and wash your hands with hot, soapy water after handling them.

PEELING TOMATOES

1. Bring a pot of water to a boil. Fill a bowl with ice water. Immerse cored tomatoes in boiling water for 30 seconds, then transfer to the ice water.

2. When the tomatoes have cooled, peel off the loosened skins. If seeding is desired, halve the tomatoes horizontally and squeeze out the seed sacs.

ROASTING AND PEELING CHILE PEPPERS OR BELL PEPPERS

1. Place the peppers in a baking dish. Broil (grill), turning as needed, until evenly blackened and blistered. Remove from the broiler (griller) and cover loosely with aluminum foil.

2. When the chiles are cool enough to handle, use your fingers or a small knife to peel off the skins. Slit or tear open the chiles to remove the seeds and white veins.

SEEDING A RAW CHILE

Using a paring knife, cut the chile in half lengthwise. With the tip of the knife, carefully cut out the white veins and the seeds attached to them. Wash your hands thoroughly.

Autumn and Winter

The hardy peak-of-season produce found in autumn and winter requires little in the way of preparation beyond peeling and cleaning. To remove the tough shells of chestnuts that arrive in markets during the cold months, however, you must first score and roast them. By contrast, the mushrooms of autumn and winter need just a quick, gentle brushing (left); you'll find special, soft-bristled mushroom brushes in well-stocked kitchen-equipment stores.

PEELING CHESTNUTS

1. Preheat an oven to 450°F (230°C). Using a sharp knife, cut a shallow X in the flat side of each chestnut. Put the chestnuts, scored sides up, in a baking pan large enough to hold them in a single layer. Pour water into the pan to form a thin layer on the bottom.

2. Bake the chestnuts until their shells begin to turn brittle and start to peel back at the X, 10–20 minutes. While the chestnuts are still warm, hold them one at a time and, starting at the X, peel away the shell and the fuzzy layer directly underneath.

CLEANING MUSHROOMS
Use a small brush with very soft bristles to gently whisk away any dirt from caps, stems, and gills. Do not rinse the mushrooms with water, as they can become soggy.

PANTRY STAPLES

No vegetarian kitchen is complete without a good supply of dried beans and rice. Follow these basic instructions for preparing them.

Cooking Beans

Before you begin to cook any dried beans, spread them out on a work surface and sort through them, discarding any stones, fibers, or misshapen or discolored specimens. Then, put them in a colander and rinse with cold running water.

Put the beans in a large bowl, add cold water to cover generously, and let stand at room temperature for 3 hours. If pressed for time, you can quick-soak the beans: Put them in a saucepan or pot, add cold water to cover generously, and bring to a simmer. Cover the pot, remove from the heat, and let stand for 1–1½ hours.

Drain the soaked beans well and return them to the saucepan or pot. Add water, vegetable stock, or other cooking liquid to cover generously. Bring slowly to a full boil, then continue boiling to neutralize the natural toxins that can cause gastric distress, briefly for lentils and peas and 10 full minutes for beans. Reduce the heat and simmer until tender. The exact cooking time will depend upon the type, age, and dryness of the beans.

Cooking Rice

The cooking method and proportions of liquid to rice will vary slightly depending upon the recipe and the type of rice you use. Follow these basic guidelines:

Basmati Rice, Jasmine Rice, and Other Long-Grain White Rice: Add 1 part rice to 1¼ parts simmering liquid and cook, covered, over very low heat until tender, about 15 minutes.

Brown Rice: Add 1 part rice to 2 parts simmering liquid and cook, covered, over very low heat until tender, 45–60 minutes.

Medium- or Short-Grain White Rice: Add 1 part rice to 1½ parts simmering liquid and cook, covered, over very low heat until tender, 15–20 minutes.

Planning Menus

All of the recipes in this book have been designed to complement one another, offering countless ways to mix and match them in vegetarian menus to suit every taste and occasion. The ten menus suggested here are intended as examples to inspire your own efforts. When planning any seasonal menu, it makes good sense to start at the market or in your garden, choosing the freshest, best-quality ingredients that you can find. (Use the lists on pages 10–11 to help you plan before you shop.) Always try to select dishes that marry well in their tastes, textures, and seasonings. Remember, too, that a widely varied diet is the key to any healthy vegetarian lifestyle.

Autumn Repast

Belgian Endive, Celery Root,
and Pear Salad with
Hazelnut Vinaigrette
PAGE 53

Butternut Squash Risotto
PAGE 71

Cranberry Crème Brûlée
PAGE 106

Pan-Asian Lunch

Rice Paper Rolls with
Peanut Sauce
PAGE 24

Crispy Noodle Pancakes
with Black Bean Sauce
PAGE 85

Passion Fruit Sorbet
PAGE 102

Southwestern Supper

Gazpacho Verde
PAGE 54

Spinach, Corn, and Potato
Enchiladas
PAGE 92

Peach and Toasted Almond
Ice Cream
PAGE 98

French Country Dinner

Parmesan Filo Napoleon
PAGE 40

Vegetarian Cassoulet
PAGE 73

Cinnamon-Poached Pears
with Blood Orange Sauce
PAGE 97

Alfresco Dinner

Spring Greens
and Flowers Salad
PAGE 37

Polenta Lasagna with
Gorgonzola Béchamel Sauce
PAGE 88

Berry Tart
with Granola Crust
PAGE 105

Mediterranean Menu

Oven-Dried Tomato
and Lentil Soup
PAGE 38

Grilled Stuffed
Portobello Mushrooms
on Porcini Couscous
PAGE 91

Coconut Biscotti
PAGE 101

Spring Garden Lunch

Fennel, Sprout,
and Herb Salad with
Lemon Vinaigrette
PAGE 47

Pizzettas with
Spring Herb Pesto
PAGE 58

Passion Fruit Sorbet
PAGE 102

Robust Winter Dinner

Yellow Pepper Soup
PAGE 44

Brown Rice and
Broccoli Rabe Pilaf
PAGE 61

Cinnamon-Poached Pears
with Blood Orange Sauce
PAGE 97

Light Summer Lunch

Fennel, Sprout,
and Herb Salad with
Lemon Vinaigrette
PAGE 47

Cold Soba Noodles
with Green Onions and
Baby Vegetables
PAGE 78

Fresh Fruit

Hearty Indian Dinner

Spicy Potato Fritters with
Green Chutney
PAGE 31

Chickpea Stew
PAGE 81

Peach and Toasted Almond
Ice Cream
PAGE 98

Lemon Cucumber, Tomato, and Mozzarella Rounds

PREP TIME: 15 MINUTES

INGREDIENTS

3 lemon cucumbers

4 plum (Roma) tomatoes

½ lb (250 g) fresh mozzarella cheese

salt and ground white pepper to taste

18 opal basil leaves

COOKING TIP: If you like, lightly drizzle the stacks of cucumber, tomato, and mozzarella with a dressing of 1 tablespoon fresh lemon juice and 3 tablespoons extra-virgin olive oil.

Two unusual ingredients—lemon cucumbers and opal basil—lend refreshing flavor to the traditional pairing of tomato and mozzarella. You can use other ingredients in their place with equally delicious results, however. Substitute 1 English (hothouse) cucumber for the small, round, and yellow lemon cucumbers and regular basil for the purple opal variety.

SERVES 6

❈ Cut the cucumbers, tomatoes, and cheese into thin slices; they should all be about the same diameter. You should have 18 slices of each.

❈ Arrange the cucumber slices in a single layer on 1 large or 2 smaller platters. Top each cucumber slice with a tomato slice and then with a mozzarella slice. Sprinkle lightly with salt and a dusting of white pepper. Garnish each stack with a basil leaf and serve.

NUTRITIONAL ANALYSIS PER SERVING: Calories 121 (Kilojoules 508); Protein 7 g; Carbohydrates 4 g; Total Fat 8 g; Saturated Fat 0 g; Cholesterol 27 mg; Sodium 30 mg; Dietary Fiber 1 g

Curried Butternut-Squash Filo Squares

PREP TIME: 40 MINUTES

COOKING TIME: 45 MINUTES

INGREDIENTS

1 butternut squash, about 1 lb (500 g)

2 shallots, minced

3 tablespoons minced fresh flat-leaf (Italian) parsley

1 tablespoon curry powder

salt and ground pepper to taste

½ cup (4 oz/125 g) unsalted butter

6 filo sheets, thawed in the refrigerator if frozen

COOKING TIP: To reduce cholesterol and saturated fat, substitute safflower oil for the butter. If you warm the oil, it will be more viscous and even less will be needed.

These sweet, spicy squash turnovers are a warm, welcoming appetizer for a holiday party. Pass a bowl of mango chutney at the table.

MAKES 8 SQUARES; SERVES 4

❈ Preheat an oven to 375°F (190°C). Line a baking sheet with parchment (baking) paper.

❈ Cut the squash in half through the stem end and scoop out and discard the seeds and fibers. Place the squash halves, cut sides down, on the prepared baking sheet. Bake until softened, 20–25 minutes. Transfer to a rack and let cool. Discard the parchment paper.

❈ Scoop the pulp from the squash into a bowl and mash with a potato masher until smooth. Stir in the shallots, parsley, and curry powder. Season with salt and pepper. Set aside.

❈ Clarify the butter: Place the butter in a frying pan and melt over medium heat. Skim off the foam from the surface. Let cool slightly, then pour off the clear yellow liquid into a clean pan; discard the white solids.

❈ Reline the baking sheet with parchment paper. Lay the stacked filo sheets on a cutting board and cut lengthwise into quarters. Cover with a damp kitchen towel to keep them from drying out, removing only a few strips at a time as needed.

❈ Lay a filo strip on a work surface. Lightly brush with clarified butter, then top with a second strip. Put 1 tablespoon squash filling near 1 end and fold the strip over 3 or 4 times to form a square. It will be open on 2 sides. Brush another strip of filo with the clarified butter and wrap it around the square over the open sides. Place the square on the prepared baking sheet. Brush lightly with butter. Repeat with the remaining filo strips and filling.

❈ Bake until golden brown, 15–18 minutes. Transfer to a serving dish and serve at once.

NUTRITIONAL ANALYSIS PER SERVING: Calories 340 (Kilojoules 714); Protein 4 g; Carbohydrates 28 g; Total Fat 24 g; Saturated Fat 14 g; Cholesterol 62 mg; Sodium 146 mg; Dietary Fiber 2 g

Camembert-Filled Artichoke Bottoms with Leek Purée

PREP TIME: 30 MINUTES

COOKING TIME: 30 MINUTES

INGREDIENTS

1 lemon, halved

6 large artichokes

2 cups (16 fl oz/500 ml) Rich Vegetable Stock (*page 9*)

3 leeks, white part only, cut into
1-inch (2.5-cm) pieces

3 tablespoons heavy (double) cream

salt and ground pepper to taste

6 oz (185 g) Camembert cheese,
rind removed

2 tomatoes, peeled, seeded, and
diced (*see technique, page 13*)

1½ teaspoons minced fresh tarragon

PREP TIP: Don't throw away all of the
leaves when preparing the artichoke
bottoms for this recipe. Instead,
steam them separately for 10 minutes and snack on them while you're
making dinner.

Start a special springtime dinner with these elegant appetizers.
Brie may be substituted for the Camembert.

SERVES 6

❊ Fill a large bowl three-fourths full with water and squeeze in the
juice of ½ lemon, then drop the lemon half into the water. Working with
1 artichoke at a time, cut off the stem even with the base and snap or
cut off all the leaves. Trim away the tough outer layer around the base.
As you work, rub the cut surfaces with the remaining lemon half, and
then drop the trimmed artichoke into the lemon water.

❊ In a saucepan over high heat, bring the stock to a boil. Add the
leeks, reduce the heat to medium, and simmer, uncovered, until very
tender, 15–20 minutes.

❊ Meanwhile, preheat an oven to 325°F (165°C). Lightly oil a baking
sheet. Bring a separate saucepan three-fourths full of water to a boil.
Drain the artichoke bottoms, add them to the boiling water, and cook
until easily pierced, 12–15 minutes. Drain and, when cool enough to
handle, gently scrape out and discard the choke from each artichoke
bottom. Place the artichoke bottoms, stem ends down, on the prepared
baking sheet.

❊ When the leeks are done, remove from the heat. Using a slotted
spoon, transfer them to a blender or food processor. Add 2–3 tablespoons of the cooking liquid and the cream and purée until smooth.
Season with salt and pepper. Cover and keep warm.

❊ Cut the Camembert cheese into 6 equal pieces. Put 1 piece on top
of each artichoke bottom. Cover with aluminum foil and place in the
oven until the cheese melts, 8–10 minutes. Remove from the oven.

❊ Spoon the leek purée onto warmed individual plates, dividing it
evenly. Place an artichoke bottom in the center of each pool of purée.
Sprinkle the tomato around each artichoke bottom. Sprinkle with the
tarragon and serve at once.

NUTRITIONAL ANALYSIS PER SERVING: Calories 259 (Kilojoules 1,088); Protein 12 g;
Carbohydrates 28 g; Total Fat 13 g; Saturated Fat 7 g; Cholesterol 31 mg; Sodium 411 mg;
Dietary Fiber 10 g

Rice Paper Rolls with Peanut Sauce

PREP TIME: 40 MINUTES, PLUS
15 MINUTES FOR SOAKING

COOKING TIME: 20 MINUTES

INGREDIENTS

FOR THE PEANUT SAUCE

½ cup (4 fl oz/125 ml) coconut milk

½ cup (5 oz/155 g) peanut butter

1 green (spring) onion, including
  tender green top, minced

1 piece lemongrass stalk, 3 inches
  (7.5 cm) long, minced

2 cloves garlic, minced

juice of ½ lime

1 tablespoon soy sauce

1 teaspoon curry powder

1 teaspoon ground coriander

½ teaspoon ground cumin

1 teaspoon chile paste, or to taste

FOR THE ROLLS

½ lb (250 g) dried rice stick noodles

3 tablespoons peanut oil

1 clove garlic, minced

½ teaspoon Asian sesame oil

½ lb (250 g) Chinese broccoli (see
  note), trimmed and coarsely
  chopped

1 carrot, peeled and coarsely grated

½ cup (1 oz/30 g) bean sprouts

24 rice paper rounds, 6 inches
  (15 cm) in diameter

fresh mint and fresh cilantro (fresh
  coriander) leaves

butter (Boston) lettuce leaves

These refreshing rolls make a great warm-weather hors d'oeuvre. At small parties, set out the filling and the rice paper rounds and let your guests assemble their own. Be sure to position a bowl of the peanut sauce alongside. If you cannot find Chinese broccoli, substitute broccoli rabe or broccoli florets.

MAKES 24 ROLLS; SERVES 8

❊ To make the sauce, in a saucepan, combine the coconut milk, peanut butter, green onion, lemongrass, garlic, lime juice, soy sauce, curry powder, coriander, and cumin. Place over medium heat and cook, stirring constantly, until well blended. Transfer to a blender or food processor and purée until smooth, thinning with water if necessary. Pour into a bowl and stir in the chile paste. Set aside.

❊ To make the rolls, in a bowl, soak the noodles in hot water to cover for 15 minutes. Drain the noodles and cut into 2-inch (5-cm) lengths. Set aside.

❊ In a wok or large frying pan over medium heat, warm the peanut oil. Add the garlic and cook, stirring, until lightly golden, about 2 minutes. Add the sesame oil, broccoli, and carrot and toss and stir until softened, 4–5 minutes. Add the noodles and toss and stir until the noodles are hot, 2–3 minutes. Add the bean sprouts, toss to mix and soften, then set aside to cool.

❊ Working with 1 rice paper round at a time, place the round on a work surface and brush liberally with water. Let stand for a minute or two until pliable. Transfer to a flat plate and place a heaping tablespoon of filling in the middle. Top with a few mint and cilantro leaves. Turn up two sides and roll into a cylinder. Continue with the remaining rounds.

❊ Line a platter with lettuce leaves and arrange the rolls on top. Serve with the peanut sauce.

NUTRITIONAL ANALYSIS PER SERVING: Calories 471 (Kilojoules 1,978); Protein 9 g; Carbohydrates 72 g; Total Fat 17 g; Saturated Fat 5 g; Cholesterol 0 mg; Sodium 293 mg; Dietary Fiber 3 g

Oven-Fried Green Tomatoes with Lemon-Ricotta Cream

PREP TIME: 20 MINUTES

COOKING TIME: 30 MINUTES

INGREDIENTS

¼ cup (1 oz/30 g) fine dried bread crumbs

olive oil as needed

¼ cup (1 oz/30 g) grated Parmesan cheese

¼ cup (1½ oz/45 g) yellow cornmeal

1 tablespoon minced fresh flat-leaf (Italian) parsley

2 teaspoons minced fresh thyme

salt and ground pepper to taste

3 eggs

½ cup (2½ oz/75 g) all-purpose (plain) flour

1 lb (500 g) green (unripened) tomatoes, cut into slices ½ inch (12 mm) thick

1 cup (8 oz/250 g) part-skim ricotta cheese

1 teaspoon grated lemon zest

If you have a vegetable garden, pick your tomatoes in early summer, when they are full size but still green, with maybe just a tinge of pink starting to show. Otherwise, green tomatoes are available seasonally in farmers' markets and at some specialty stores. Halved green cherry tomatoes can be baked and topped in the same manner. Garnish with additional strips of lemon zest, if desired.

SERVES 6

❁ Preheat an oven to 350°F (180°C). Spread the bread crumbs in a small pan and toast in the oven until lightly browned, about 8 minutes. Transfer to a shallow bowl and let cool.

❁ Reduce the oven temperature to 325°F (165°C). Coat a baking sheet with a thin layer of olive oil.

❁ Add the Parmesan cheese, cornmeal, parsley, and thyme to the bread crumbs and stir to mix. Season with salt and pepper. In another bowl, beat the eggs until blended. Place the flour in a third bowl.

❁ One at a time, dip the tomato slices into the flour, lightly dusting both sides. Then dip into the eggs and immediately into the crumb mixture, coating both sides well. Place slightly apart on the prepared baking sheet.

❁ Bake until golden brown on top, about 15 minutes. Remove from the oven and turn over the slices with a spatula. Return to the oven until golden brown on the second side, about 10 minutes longer.

❁ Meanwhile, place the ricotta in a bowl and, using an electric mixer, whip until light and smooth. Mix in the lemon zest and season lightly with salt and pepper.

❁ Transfer the tomatoes to a warmed platter and top each slice with a dollop of the ricotta cream. Serve warm.

NUTRITIONAL ANALYSIS PER SERVING: Calories 224 (Kilojoules 941); Protein 13 g; Carbohydrates 24 g; Total Fat 8 g; Saturated Fat 4 g; Cholesterol 122 mg; Sodium 218 mg; Dietary Fiber 1 g

Vegetable Samosas

PREP TIME: 35 MINUTES, PLUS
30 MINUTES FOR CHILLING

COOKING TIME: 55 MINUTES

INGREDIENTS

2 large baking potatoes, peeled and
cut into 2-inch (5-cm) pieces

1 teaspoon curry powder

6 tablespoons (3 fl oz/90 ml)
vegetable oil

½ cup (2 oz/60 g) chopped yellow
onion

1 carrot, peeled and coarsely grated

½ cup (2½ oz/75 g) shelled peas

3 tablespoons minced fresh cilantro
(fresh coriander)

salt and ground pepper to taste

1 package (17¼ oz/537 g) frozen puff
pastry, thawed in the refrigerator

1 egg beaten with 1 tablespoon
water

2 teaspoons caraway seeds

COOKING TIP: Prepare the samosas
as directed, but do not bake. Spread
on a baking sheet and freeze, then
transfer to lock-top plastic freezer
bags and store in the freezer for up
to 3 months. To bake, transfer to a
parchment-lined baking sheet, brush
with the egg wash, and sprinkle with
the caraway seeds. Increase the baking time by 3 minutes.

Wonderful with fresh spring peas, these crisp, Indian-style
turnovers can be made with your choice of vegetables in other
seasons. Serve them with the green chutney that accompanies
the Spicy Potato Fritters on page 31, or offer them alongside
Chickpea Stew (page 81).

MAKES ABOUT 2 DOZEN SAMOSAS; SERVES 12

❈ Place the potatoes in a saucepan with water to cover and bring to a
boil over high heat. Cook until very tender, 20–25 minutes. Drain and
transfer to a bowl. Using a fork, mash well, mixing in the curry powder
and 3 tablespoons of the oil at the same time. Set aside.

❈ In a sauté pan over medium heat, warm the remaining 3 tablespoons
oil. Add the onion and sauté until softened, 3–4 minutes. Add the carrot
and sauté until the carrot has softened, 3–4 minutes longer. Stir the
onion and carrot into the potatoes. Bring a small saucepan three-fourths
full of water to a boil, add the peas, and blanch for 1 minute. Drain and
add to the potato mixture along with the cilantro. Mix well and season
with salt and pepper. Set aside to cool.

❈ On a work surface, roll out the puff pastry very thin. Using a scal-
loped biscuit cutter 3 inches (7.5 cm) in diameter, cut out rounds. Place
about 1 teaspoon of the potato mixture in the center of each round.
Brush the edges of the round with the egg-water mixture, fold in half,
and press the edges together to seal.

❈ Preheat an oven to 400°F (200°C). Line a baking sheet with parchment (baking) paper.

❈ Place the filled pastries on the prepared baking sheet and brush with
the remaining egg-water mixture. Sprinkle the tops with the caraway
seeds. Cover and chill for 30 minutes.

❈ Bake the samosas until golden brown, 15–18 minutes. Serve hot.

NUTRITIONAL ANALYSIS PER SERVING: Calories 336 (Kilojoules 1,411); Protein 5 g;
Carbohydrates 28 g; Total Fat 23 g; Saturated Fat 3 g; Cholesterol 18 mg; Sodium 112 mg;
Dietary Fiber 2 g

Spicy Potato Fritters with Green Chutney

PREP TIME: 20 MINUTES

COOKING TIME: 30 MINUTES

INGREDIENTS

FOR THE GREEN CHUTNEY

3 cups (3 oz/90 g) fresh cilantro
(fresh coriander) leaves

¼ cup (¼ oz/7 g) fresh mint leaves

1–3 serrano chiles, seeded and
coarsely chopped

1 piece fresh ginger, ½ inch (12 mm),
peeled and coarsely chopped

1 clove garlic

½ cup (4 fl oz/125 ml) water

juice of ½ lime

1 teaspoon sugar, or to taste

salt

FOR THE FRITTERS

1 cup (5½ oz/170 g) chickpea
(garbanzo bean) flour

1 cup (8 fl oz/250 ml) Vegetable
Stock (*page 9*) or water

1 tablespoon peanut oil, plus oil for
frying

1 tablespoon garam masala (*see note*)

½ teaspoon ground turmeric

½ teaspoon baking powder

2 green (spring) onions, minced

1 serrano chile, minced

2 tablespoons minced fresh cilantro
(fresh coriander)

salt and ground pepper to taste

1 yam or sweet potato

1 baking potato

Garam masala is an Indian spice blend found in stores specializing in Indian foods and shops with an international selection. You can also make your own: Combine 1 cinnamon stick, 4 whole cloves, seeds from 5 cardamom pods, and 1 tablespoon each cumin seeds, coriander seeds, and peppercorns in a dry non-stick frying pan over medium heat. Toast, shaking the pan occasionally, until aromatic and darkened slightly, about 5 minutes. Let cool, then grind in a spice mill to a fine consistency. Store in a tightly sealed jar at room temperature for up to 6 months.

SERVES 8

❀ Preheat an oven to 250°F (120°C).

❀ To make the chutney, in a blender or food processor, combine the cilantro, mint, chiles, ginger, garlic, water, lime juice, sugar, and salt to taste. Purée until smooth. Add more water if needed to achieve a good consistency. Taste and adjust the seasonings. You should have about 1¼ cups (10 fl oz/310 ml). Set aside.

❀ To make the fritters, in a bowl, combine the chickpea flour, stock, 1 tablespoon peanut oil, garam masala, turmeric, and baking powder. Stir until well mixed. Stir in the green onions, chile, and cilantro. The batter should be thick. Season with salt and pepper.

❀ Pour peanut oil into a large frying pan to a depth of 1 inch (2.5 cm) and heat over medium heat to 350°F (180°C) on a deep-fat frying thermometer. Meanwhile, peel and thinly slice the yam or sweet potato and the baking potato. Working in batches, dip the slices into the batter to coat and then slip them into the hot oil. Fry, turning once, until golden brown on both sides, 3–5 minutes on each side. Using a slotted spoon or tongs, transfer to paper towels to drain. Keep warm until all are done.

❀ Transfer to a warmed serving platter and serve with the chutney.

NUTRITIONAL ANALYSIS PER SERVING: Calories 203 (Kilojoules 853); Protein 5 g; Carbohydrates 24 g; Total Fat 10 g; Saturated Fat 2 g; Cholesterol 0 mg; Sodium 43 mg; Dietary Fiber 3 g

Red Cabbage Rolls

PREP TIME: 30 MINUTES

COOKING TIME: 45 MINUTES

INGREDIENTS

1 head red cabbage

ice water as needed

¼ cup (2 fl oz/60 ml) vegetable oil

½ cup (2 oz/60 g) chopped yellow
onion

2 cloves garlic, minced

1½ cups (12 fl oz/375 ml) Rich
Vegetable Stock (page 9)

¼ cup (2 fl oz/60 ml) tomato sauce

¾ cup (5 oz/155 g) jasmine rice or
other long-grain white rice

1 teaspoon red pepper flakes, or to
taste

¼ cup (⅓ oz/10 g) minced fresh
flat-leaf (Italian) parsley

3 tablespoons minced fresh cilantro
(fresh coriander)

½ teaspoon ground cumin

¼ teaspoon ground coriander

salt and ground pepper to taste

These rolls are delicious served at room temperature accompanied with sour cream that has been seasoned with a little minced cilantro. To serve them as a main course, place in a baking dish, cover with a tomato sauce, and bake in a 375°F (190°C) oven to heat through.

MAKES 16 ROLLS; SERVES 8

❀ Remove the tough outer leaves of the cabbage and discard. Cut out the core but leave the head whole.

❀ Bring a large pot three-fourths full of water to a boil. Immerse the cabbage in the boiling water and cook until the leaves are pliable and separate easily when gently pulled apart with tongs, 5–7 minutes. Drain and immerse immediately in ice water to stop the cooking. Drain again and blot dry with paper towels. Carefully pull apart and set aside 16 large leaves.

❀ In a saucepan over medium heat, warm the vegetable oil. Add the onion and garlic and sauté until lightly golden, 4–5 minutes. Add the stock, tomato sauce, rice, and red pepper flakes and bring to a boil. Cover, reduce the heat to low, and cook until the rice is tender, about 30 minutes.

❀ Remove the pan from the heat, add the parsley, cilantro, cumin, and coriander and mix well. Season with salt and pepper and set aside to cool.

❀ Trim off the heavy rib from the base of each cabbage leaf, squaring off the end. Place a heaping tablespoon of the filling in the center of the leaf and, starting from the rib end, roll up the leaf, tucking in the sides and forming a cylinder.

❀ Place the rolls, seam sides down, on a serving platter. Serve at room temperature.

NUTRITIONAL ANALYSIS PER SERVING: Calories 176 (Kilojoules 739); Protein 3 g; Carbohydrates 23 g; Total Fat 9 g; Saturated Fat 1 g; Cholesterol 0 mg; Sodium 62 mg; Dietary Fiber 3 g

Grilled Summer Heirloom Vegetables with Black Bean Salsa

PREP TIME: 30 MINUTES, PLUS
3 HOURS FOR SOAKING

COOKING TIME: 1¼ HOURS,
PLUS PREPARING FIRE

INGREDIENTS

1⅛ cups (8 oz/250 g) dried black beans

3 cups (24 fl oz/750 ml) Vegetable
Stock (page 9)

½ cup (2½ oz/75 g) finely chopped
yellow onion

1 carrot, peeled and finely diced

1 celery stalk, sliced

1 cup (6 oz/185 g) corn kernels

1 tablespoon olive oil

½ cup (1½ oz/45 g) thinly sliced
green (spring) onion

1 red bell pepper (capsicum), diced

2 cloves garlic, minced

1 jalapeño chile, seeded and minced

1 teaspoon ground cumin

salt and ground pepper to taste

½ cup (½ oz/15 g) fresh cilantro
(fresh coriander) leaves

olive oil

1 red (Spanish) onion, cut into wedges

1 Asian (slender) eggplant (aubergine),
sliced

1 zucchini (courgette), sliced

1 fennel bulb, trimmed and cut
lengthwise into 8 wedges

8 mushrooms, stemmed

8 cherry tomatoes

16 cloves garlic, peeled

Heirloom vegetables are what your grandmother grew in her garden—tomatoes that taste like tomatoes and peppers that are sweet and delicious. They were phased out due to low yields, but their wonderful flavors are helping them make a comeback in backyards and at farmers' markets. Look for varieties such as Pimiento Ruffled red bell peppers, Italian White eggplants, Cocozelle zucchini, and Peacevine cherry tomatoes. If desired, pass tortilla chips for scooping up extra salsa.

SERVES 4

❀ Pick over the beans and discard any damaged beans or impurities. Rinse, place in a bowl, and add water to cover generously. Let soak for 3 hours. Drain and place in a saucepan along with the stock, onion, carrot, and celery. Bring to a boil, then reduce the heat to low and simmer, uncovered, until tender but not mushy, about 1 hour.

❀ Meanwhile, bring a saucepan three-fourths full of water to a boil, add the corn and blanch for 30 seconds. Drain and set aside.

❀ When the beans are ready, drain and rinse in cold water to cool, then drain again and place in a bowl. Add the olive oil and toss well. Add the green onion, bell pepper, garlic, jalapeño chile, and corn and toss again to make a salsa. Season with the cumin and salt and pepper. Sprinkle with the cilantro. Set aside until ready to serve.

❀ Soak 8 wooden skewers in water to cover for at least 15 minutes. Meanwhile, prepare a fire in a grill. Lightly brush the grill rack with olive oil. Alternatively, preheat a broiler (griller).

❀ Thread the onion, eggplant, zucchini, fennel, mushrooms, tomatoes, and garlic onto the skewers, alternating them and dividing them evenly. Place the skewers on the grill rack about 4 inches (10 cm) above the fire, or on a broiler pan. Brush lightly with olive oil, and season with salt and pepper. Grill or broil, turning as needed, until lightly browned, about 10 minutes.

❀ Transfer the skewers to a serving platter. Serve with the salsa.

NUTRITIONAL ANALYSIS PER SERVING: Calories 502 (Kilojoules 2,108); Protein 20 g; Carbohydrates 70 g; Total Fat 19 g; Saturated Fat 3 g; Cholesterol 0 mg; Sodium 125 mg; Dietary Fiber 14 g

Spring Greens and Flowers Salad

PREP TIME: 15 MINUTES

INGREDIENTS

4 cups (4 oz/125 g) baby spinach
leaves

4 cups (4 oz/125 g) oakleaf lettuce
leaves

1 cup (1 oz/30 g) mâche leaves

½ cup (¾ oz/20 g) garlic chive
flowers or 2 tablespoons snipped
fresh chives

¼ cup (2 fl oz/60 ml) unseasoned
rice vinegar

2 tablespoons minced fresh young
ginger

1 clove garlic, minced

½ cup (4 fl oz/125 ml) safflower oil

salt and ground pepper to taste

12 pesticide-free nasturtiums

Celebrate spring with this colorful, simple-to-make salad. You can buy edible, pesticide-free flowers at many greengrocers and farmers' markets, or grow some in your garden at home. Other pretty, edible flowers include pansies, violets, hibiscuses, and scented geraniums. If young ginger is unavailable, substitute 1 tablespoon peeled and minced fresh mature ginger.

SERVES 6

✾ In a large bowl, combine the spinach, oakleaf lettuce, mâche, and chive flowers or chives. Toss gently to mix and set aside.

✾ In a small bowl, combine the rice vinegar, ginger, and garlic. While whisking continuously, slowly drizzle in the safflower oil to form a vinaigrette. Season with salt and pepper.

✾ Drizzle the vinaigrette over the greens and toss to mix well. Transfer to a salad bowl, garnish with the nasturtiums, and serve at once.

NUTRITIONAL ANALYSIS PER SERVING: Calories 171 (Kilojoules 718); Protein 1 g; Carbohydrates 2 g; Total Fat 18 g; Saturated Fat 2 g; Cholesterol 0 mg; Sodium 17 mg; Dietary Fiber 1 g

Oven-Dried Tomato and Lentil Soup

PREP TIME: 15 MINUTES, PLUS
2 HOURS FOR DRYING

COOKING TIME: 1 HOUR

INGREDIENTS

6 plum (Roma) tomatoes, quartered
lengthwise

coarse sea salt

1½ cups (10½ oz/330 g) dried green
lentils

3 tablespoons extra-virgin olive oil

1 yellow onion, minced

1 carrot, peeled and minced

1 celery stalk, minced

6 cups (48 fl oz/1.5 l) Rich Vegetable
Stock (page 9)

1 lb (500 g) red new potatoes,
unpeeled, quartered

1 tablespoon minced fresh rosemary

salt and ground pepper to taste

PREP TIP: You can use 12 dry-packed
sun-dried tomatoes in place of the
oven-dried tomatoes. Soak them in 1½
cups (12 fl oz/375 ml) warm stock or
warm water for 20 minutes. Drain,
reserving the soaking liquid, and
proceed as instructed in the recipe.
Use the reserved soaking liquid in
place of 1½ cups (12 fl oz/375 ml) of
the Rich Vegetable Stock.

If you are lucky enough to have a vegetable garden that yields
a big tomato harvest, you can dehydrate the excess in the oven
as directed in this recipe and use them later in soups and stews.
The tomatoes taste best if they are still a bit moist and pliable
when dried. Store any you don't use in the freezer. They will
keep for up to 3 months.

SERVES 6

❀ Preheat an oven to 250°F (120°C). Place the tomatoes, cut sides up, on
a rack set on a baking sheet. Sprinkle with sea salt and place in the oven
for about 2 hours. The tomatoes will dehydrate and intensify in flavor,
but should still be a little soft. Remove from the oven and set aside.

❀ Meanwhile, pick over the lentils and discard any damaged lentils
or impurities. Rinse the lentils. Place in a bowl and add water to cover
generously. Let soak for 1 hour. Drain and set aside.

❀ In a saucepan over medium heat, warm the olive oil. Add the onion,
carrot, and celery and sauté until golden brown, 5–7 minutes. Add the
stock, drained lentils, and potatoes and bring to a boil. Reduce the heat
to low and simmer, uncovered, until the lentils and potatoes are tender,
30–40 minutes.

❀ Add the reserved tomatoes and the rosemary and continue to simmer,
stirring gently to retain the shape of the tomatoes, until the flavors have
blended, about 15 minutes longer. Season with salt and pepper.

❀ Ladle into warmed bowls and serve hot.

NUTRITIONAL ANALYSIS PER SERVING: Calories 381 (Kilojoules 1,600); Protein 16 g;
Carbohydrates 49 g; Total Fat 15 g; Saturated Fat 2 g; Cholesterol 0 mg; Sodium 154 mg;
Dietary Fiber 9 g

Parmesan Filo Napoleon

PREP TIME: 30 MINUTES

COOKING TIME: 25 MINUTES

INGREDIENTS

½ cup (4 oz/125 g) unsalted butter

6 filo sheets, thawed in the
   refrigerator if frozen

¾ cup (3 oz/90 g) finely grated
   Parmesan cheese

2 teaspoons red wine vinegar

I egg yolk

I teaspoon Dijon mustard

½ cup (4 fl oz/125 ml) plus 3 tablespoons extra-virgin olive oil

salt and ground pepper to taste

I cup (6 oz/185 g) corn kernels

ice water as needed

3 baking potatoes, peeled and thinly
   sliced

3 cups (3 oz/90 g) spinach leaves,
   shredded

PREP TIP: Filo can often be found in
the freezer section of a well-stocked
food store. To thaw, leave it overnight
in the refrigerator, then remove it
from the refrigerator I hour before
opening the airtight package. Leftover
sheets of filo can be wrapped airtight
with plastic wrap and refrigerated
for up to 3 days.

To keep the filo crisp, assemble the layers of this elegant first
course just before serving.

SERVES 8

❊ Preheat an oven to 375°F (190°C). Line 2 baking sheets with parchment (baking) paper.

❊ Clarify the butter: Place the butter in a frying pan and melt over
medium heat. Skim off the foam from the surface. Let cool slightly, then
pour off the clear yellow liquid into a clean pan; discard the white solids.

❊ Working with I filo sheet at a time and keeping the others covered
with a damp kitchen towel to prevent drying, lay the sheet on a cutting
board. Brush with the clarified butter and sprinkle with about 2 tablespoons of the cheese. Repeat with 2 more filo sheets, stacking them on
top of the first. Cut lengthwise into quarters, then cut crosswise into
quarters, creating 16 rectangles each measuring about 3½ inches by
4½ inches (9 cm by 11.5 cm). Place on a prepared baking sheet. Repeat
with 3 more filo sheets and place on the second baking sheet. Bake until
golden brown, 8–10 minutes. Let cool on the baking sheets.

❊ Meanwhile, in a small bowl, whisk together the vinegar, egg yolk, and
mustard. While whisking constantly, drizzle in the ½ cup (4 fl oz/125 ml)
olive oil to form a vinaigrette. Season with salt and pepper. Set aside.

❊ Bring a small saucepan three-fourths full of water to a boil. Add the
corn, blanch for 2 minutes, and drain. Quickly immerse in ice water and
drain again. Set aside. Refill the saucepan and blanch the potato slices
for 30 seconds. Drain, immerse in ice water, and drain again. Pat dry.

❊ In a sauté pan over medium heat, warm the remaining 3 tablespoons
olive oil. Add the potatoes, season liberally with salt and pepper, and
sauté until golden brown and tender, 7–9 minutes. Using a slotted
spoon, transfer to paper towels to drain briefly, then place in a bowl.
Add the spinach and corn, drizzle on the vinaigrette, and toss well.

❊ To assemble the napoleons, place I filo rectangle on each individual
plate. Top with a spoonful of the potato-corn mixture. Repeat the layers
twice, then top with with a filo rectangle. Serve at once.

NUTRITIONAL ANALYSIS PER SERVING: Calories 406 (Kilojoules 1,705); Protein 7 g;
Carbohydrates 24 g; Total Fat 33 g; Saturated Fat 10 g; Cholesterol 56 mg; Sodium 271 mg;
Dietary Fiber 2 g

Three-Bean Salad with Toasted Coriander Vinaigrette

PREP TIME: 20 MINUTES, PLUS
1 HOUR FOR MARINATING

COOKING TIME: 35 MINUTES

INGREDIENTS

½ lb (250 g) fresh flageolet beans or other fresh shelling beans, shelled

ice water as needed

1 lb (500 g) yellow wax beans, trimmed and cut into 2-inch (5-cm) lengths

1 lb (500 g) haricots verts, trimmed

1 teaspoon ground coriander

¼ cup (2 fl oz/60 ml) lemon juice

2 tablespoons white wine vinegar

2 shallots, minced

¾ cup (6 fl oz/180 ml) safflower oil

1 teaspoon grated lemon zest

salt and ground pepper to taste

Three-bean salad is an old-fashioned summertime favorite. Here is an updated version that calls for fresh shelling beans, slender French snap beans, and pale wax beans. You can substitute other green beans for the haricots verts. The flavor intensifies if the salad is allowed to marinate for at least 1 hour.

SERVES 6–8

❊ Bring a large saucepan three-fourths full of salted water to a boil. Add the shelling beans and boil until just tender, 10–15 minutes. Scoop out with a slotted spoon and immediately immerse in ice water to stop the cooking. Scoop out of the ice water and set aside to drain. Repeat with the yellow wax beans and haricots verts, cooking the wax beans 7–8 minutes and the haricots verts about 5 minutes.

❊ In a small, dry frying pan over medium heat, toast the coriander, shaking the pan occasionally, until aromatic, 2–3 minutes. Transfer to a plate to cool.

❊ In a small bowl, combine the lemon juice, vinegar, and shallots. While whisking continuously, slowly drizzle in the safflower oil to form a vinaigrette. Stir in the lemon zest and coriander, and season with salt and pepper.

❊ Combine all the beans in a large mixing bowl. Add the vinaigrette and toss to mix well. Let stand for at least 1 hour to marinate, or refrigerate for up to 3 hours. Serve at room temperature or chilled.

NUTRITIONAL ANALYSIS PER SERVING: Calories 254 (Kilojoules 1,067); Protein 3 g; Carbohydrates 11 g; Total Fat 24 g; Saturated Fat 2 g; Cholesterol 0 mg; Sodium 15 mg; Dietary Fiber 2 g

Yellow Pepper Soup

PREP TIME: 15 MINUTES

COOKING TIME: 55 MINUTES

INGREDIENTS

¼ cup (2 fl oz/60 ml) olive oil

1 yellow onion, diced

1 carrot, peeled and minced

1 celery stalk, diced

6 cups (48 fl oz/1.5 l) Vegetable
Stock (page 9)

8 large yellow bell peppers
(capsicums), halved and seeded

1 teaspoon minced fresh thyme

salt and ground pepper to taste

6–12 fresh flat-leaf (Italian) parsley
leaves

SERVING TIP: For a special-occasion
dinner, make half the recipe with
yellow peppers and half the recipe
with red. Then simultaneously and
carefully pour the two soups into
each bowl from opposite sides, so
that each color fills half the bowl.

This soup is best during the summer months, when bell peppers are at their peak of flavor. For a completely different taste, make it with roasted and peeled bell peppers (see technique, page 13), reducing the cooking time to 15–20 minutes. Red peppers also make a beautiful soup.

SERVES 6

❋ In a large saucepan over medium heat, warm the olive oil. Add the onion, carrot, and celery and sauté, stirring constantly, until golden brown, 5–7 minutes.

❋ Add the stock, raise the heat to high, and bring to a boil. Add the peppers, reduce the heat to medium, cover, and simmer until the peppers are very tender, 30–35 minutes. Remove from the heat.

❋ Working in batches, and using a slotted spoon, transfer the peppers, onion, carrot, and celery to a blender or food processor. Add some of the cooking liquid and purée until smooth. Return to the saucepan and place over medium heat.

❋ Add the thyme, bring to a simmer, and cook, uncovered, for 10 minutes to blend the flavors. Season with salt and pepper.

❋ Ladle into warmed soup bowls or mugs and garnish each bowl with 1 or 2 parsley leaves. Serve at once.

NUTRITIONAL ANALYSIS PER SERVING: Calories 177 (Kilojoules 743); Protein 2 g; Carbohydrates 13 g; Total Fat 14 g; Saturated Fat 2 g; Cholesterol 0 mg; Sodium 18 mg; Dietary Fiber 3 g

Fennel, Sprout, and Herb Salad with Lemon Vinaigrette

PREP TIME: 15 MINUTES

INGREDIENTS

2 fennel bulbs

2 cups (4 oz/125 g) assorted sprouts such as sunflower, radish, onion, and clover

1 bunch watercress, tough stems removed

¼ cup (⅓ oz/10 g) fresh chervil leaves

1 bunch fresh chives, snipped

1 bunch radishes, trimmed and coarsely grated

¼ cup (2 fl oz/60 ml) lemon juice

¼ cup (2 fl oz/60 ml) champagne vinegar

¾ cup (6 fl oz/180 ml) safflower oil

1 teaspoon grated lemon zest

salt and ground white pepper to taste

If you cannot easily find chervil, substitute parsley or another complementary herb such as tarragon. Use alfalfa sprouts in place of the assorted sprouts, if you like, although variety makes a more interesting salad.

SERVES 6

✤ Cut off the stems and feathery tops and any bruised outer stalks from the fennel bulbs. Reserve the stems and tops for another use. Coarsely chop the bulbs and place in a bowl along with the sprouts, watercress, chervil, chives, and radishes. Toss to mix well.

✤ In a small bowl, combine the lemon juice and vinegar. While whisking continuously, slowly drizzle in the safflower oil to form a vinaigrette. Stir in the lemon zest, and season with salt and white pepper.

✤ Drizzle the vinaigrette over the fennel and herb mixture, tossing to mix well. Serve at room temperature.

NUTRITIONAL ANALYSIS PER SERVING: Calories 273 (Kilojoules 1,147); Protein 3 g; Carbohydrates 6 g; Total Fat 28 g; Saturated Fat 2 g; Cholesterol 0 mg; Sodium 120 mg; Dietary Fiber 2 g

Hearty Borscht with Horseradish-Dill Sour Cream

PREP TIME: 20 MINUTES

COOKING TIME: 30 MINUTES

INGREDIENTS

6 beets with greens attached, about
    2 lb (1 kg) total weight

6 cups (48 fl oz/1.5 l) Rich Vegetable
    Stock (page 9)

¼ cup (2 fl oz/60 ml) tomato sauce

2 celery stalks, sliced

2 carrots, peeled and grated

1 yellow onion, chopped

1 baking potato, peeled and diced

salt and ground pepper to taste

½ cup (4 fl oz/125 ml) sour cream

1 tablespoon minced fresh dill

1 teaspoon bottled prepared
    horseradish

Although borscht is often served chilled, this version is at its best piping hot for lunch or dinner on a rainy autumn day. Roasting the beets brings out their natural sweetness, and the beet greens add an extra measure of flavor, texture, and nutrition.

SERVES 8

✸ Preheat an oven to 400°F (200°C). Lightly oil a baking sheet.

✸ Trim off the beet greens and set aside. Quarter the beets lengthwise and place on the prepared baking sheet. Roast until softened and lightly browned, 15–20 minutes. Remove from the oven and let cool. Peel and cut into bite-sized chunks. Thinly slice enough beet greens to measure 1 cup (3 oz/90 g). Set aside.

✸ In a saucepan over medium heat, combine the stock, tomato sauce, celery, carrots, onion, and potato. Bring to a boil over medium heat, reduce the heat to low, and simmer, uncovered, until the vegetables are tender, about 20 minutes. Add the beets and beet greens and simmer until the beets are tender and the greens are wilted, about 10 minutes longer. Season with salt and pepper.

✸ Meanwhile, in a small bowl, stir together the sour cream, dill, and horseradish until blended.

✸ To serve, ladle the soup into warmed bowls and top each with a spoonful of the sour cream mixture. Serve immediately.

NUTRITIONAL ANALYSIS PER SERVING: Calories 147 (Kilojoules 617); Protein 3 g; Carbohydrates 16 g; Total Fat 9 g; Saturated Fat 3 g; Cholesterol 6 mg; Sodium 164 mg; Dietary Fiber 2 g

Hot-and-Sour Coconut Milk Soup

PREP TIME: 15 MINUTES

COOKING TIME: 20 MINUTES

INGREDIENTS

2 cups (16 fl oz/500 ml) coconut milk

2 cups (16 fl oz/500 ml) Rich Vegetable Stock (*page 9*)

6 small dried red chiles, seeded

3 cloves garlic, crushed

1 lemongrass stalk, tops discarded and white bulb pounded flat, then cut into ½-inch (12-mm) slices

¼ lb (125 g) small oyster mushrooms, brushed clean and stemmed

1 teaspoon finely grated lime zest

2 green (spring) onions, including tender green tops, sliced

½ cup (1 oz/30 g) bean sprouts

juice of 1 lime

ground pepper to taste

This Asian-inspired soup has a brisk spiciness that is wonderfully refreshing on a hot summer's day. Adjust the soup's heat to your taste by increasing or decreasing the number of chiles.

SERVES 4

✳ In a saucepan over medium heat, combine the coconut milk, stock, chiles, garlic, and lemongrass. Bring to a boil, then reduce the heat to medium-low. Simmer, uncovered, for 15 minutes to infuse the stock with the lemongrass and garlic.

✳ Add the mushrooms and lime zest, and cook until the mushrooms are tender and the flavors are blended, about 5 minutes longer.

✳ Just before serving, add the green onions, bean sprouts, and lime juice. Remove from the heat and season with pepper.

✳ Ladle into warmed bowls and serve immediately.

NUTRITIONAL ANALYSIS PER SERVING: Calories 267 (Kilojoules 1,121); Protein 4 g; Carbohydrates 9 g; Total Fat 27 g; Saturated Fat 21 g; Cholesterol 0 mg; Sodium 21 mg; Dietary Fiber 2 g

PREP TIP: If oyster mushrooms are unavailable, use 1 can (15 oz/470 g) straw mushrooms instead. Drain and rinse the straw mushrooms before you add them to the soup.

Belgian Endive, Celery Root, and Pear Salad with Hazelnut Vinaigrette

PREP TIME: 15 MINUTES

COOKING TIME: 10 MINUTES

INGREDIENTS

½ cup (2½ oz/75 g) hazelnuts (filberts)

2 tablespoons sherry wine vinegar

1 shallot, minced

½ cup (4 fl oz/125 ml) hazelnut oil
  or vegetable oil

salt and ground pepper to taste

5 heads Belgian endive (chicory/
  witloof)

1 celery root (celeriac), peeled and
  coarsely grated

1 head radicchio, shredded

2 pears (see note)

1 lemon, halved

COOKING TIP: To make your own hazelnut-infused oil, combine ½ cup (2½ oz/75 g) chopped, toasted hazelnuts with 1 cup (8 fl oz/250 ml) vegetable oil in a small saucepan. Warm over medium heat for 10 minutes. Remove from the heat and let stand for 30 minutes, then strain.

This rich salad is an excellent beginning to an autumn meal. Select Bosc or Anjou pears that are ripe, yet still firm to the touch. Once you have grated the celery root, toss it with the vinaigrette to keep it from turning brown.

SERVES 4

❀ Preheat an oven to 350°F (180°C). Spread the hazelnuts on a baking sheet and toast until fragrant and the skins have loosened, 5–7 minutes. While still warm, transfer to a kitchen towel. Rub the towel vigorously to remove the skins; do not worry if small bits remain. Coarsely chop and set aside.

❀ In a bowl, combine the vinegar and shallot. While whisking continuously, slowly drizzle in the hazelnut or vegetable oil to form a vinaigrette. Season with salt and pepper. Set aside.

❀ Separate the leaves from the Belgian endive. Cut them lengthwise into long, narrow strips and place in a bowl. Add the celery root, radicchio, and all but 2 tablespoons of the vinaigrette. Toss to coat evenly, then divide among chilled individual plates.

❀ Peel, halve, and core each pear, leaving the stems intact, if desired. Place each half, flat side down, on a cutting board and cut lengthwise into thin slices, leaving the slices attached at the stem end. Rub the cut surfaces with the lemon halves to prevent browning, then fan each pear half atop a mound of greens. Drizzle evenly with the reserved vinaigrette, sprinkle with the hazelnuts, and serve.

NUTRITIONAL ANALYSIS PER SERVING: Calories 457 (Kilojoules 1,919); Protein 5 g; Carbohydrates 28 g; Total Fat 39 g; Saturated Fat 3 g; Cholesterol 0 mg; Sodium 99 mg; Dietary Fiber 5 g

Gazpacho Verde

PREP TIME: 20 MINUTES, PLUS
2 HOURS FOR CHILLING

COOKING TIME: 30 MINUTES

INGREDIENTS

1 lb (500 g) tomatillos, husks
  removed

1 yellow onion, sliced

2 jalapeño chiles, halved and seeded

¼ cup (1 oz/30 g) walnuts

1 green bell pepper (capsicum),
  seeded and coarsely chopped

1 English (hothouse) cucumber,
  peeled and coarsely chopped

2 cloves garlic

2 tablespoons olive oil

juice of 1 lime

1 tablespoon minced fresh flat-leaf
  (Italian) parsley

salt and ground black pepper to taste

cayenne pepper to taste

1 jicama, peeled and diced

Here, tomatillos stand in for the ripe red tomatoes that are the usual base for this cold summer soup from Spain. Toasted walnuts take the place of the bread that thickens the soup. Green tomatoes make an interesting substitute for the tomatillos. For a sweet flavor boost, roast 6–8 peeled garlic cloves along with the tomatillos and purée them with the other ingredients.

SERVES 6

❀ Preheat an oven to 375°F (190°C). Lightly oil a baking sheet.

❀ Place the tomatillos, onion slices, and jalapeños on the prepared baking sheet. Roast until lightly browned and softened, 18–20 minutes. Remove from the oven and let cool.

❀ Reduce the oven temperature to 350°F (180°C). Spread the walnuts on another, ungreased baking sheet and toast until fragrant and just beginning to brown, 5–7 minutes. Remove from the oven and let cool.

❀ Place the cooled vegetables and nuts in a blender or food processor along with the bell pepper, cucumber, garlic, olive oil, lime juice, and parsley. Process until smooth. Transfer to a nonaluminum bowl and season with salt, black pepper, and cayenne pepper. Cover and chill for at least 2 hours or for up to 3 hours.

❀ Ladle into chilled bowls and garnish each serving with a spoonful of diced jicama. Serve immediately.

NUTRITIONAL ANALYSIS PER SERVING: Calories 150 (Kilojoules 630); Protein 3 g; Carbohydrates 17 g; Total Fat 9 g; Saturated Fat 1 g; Cholesterol 0 mg; Sodium 8 mg; Dietary Fiber 5 g

Angel Hair Pasta with Spring Vegetables

PREP TIME: 30 MINUTES

COOKING TIME: 35 MINUTES

INGREDIENTS

2 lb (1 kg) fava (broad) beans

1 bunch baby carrots (about 6 oz/
185 g), trimmed, peeled, and
halved lengthwise

ice water as needed

½ lb (250 g) asparagus, tough ends
removed, cut into 2-inch (5-cm)
lengths

½ lb (250 g) sugar snap peas, trimmed

1 lb (500 g) angel hair pasta

6 tablespoons (3 fl oz/90 ml) olive oil

1 yellow onion, diced

3 cups (24 fl oz/750 ml) Rich
Vegetable Stock (page 9)

salt and ground pepper to taste

½ pint (6 oz/185 g) yellow
pear tomatoes, halved lengthwise

½ cup (½ oz/15 g) fresh basil leaves,
shredded

2 oz (60 g) Parmesan cheese, grated
or shaved with a vegetable peeler

COOKING TIP: Blanching vegetables
helps them retain their brilliant colors.
Boil them just long enough to soften
slightly; the timing varies with the
size and type of vegetable. Always
immediately immerse the blanched
vegetables in ice water to stop the
cooking, then drain well.

The best seasonal vegetables star in this simple pasta dish. The angel hair pasta, also known as capellini, is very thin and cooks quickly, so be careful not to overcook it.

SERVES 6

❀ Shell the fava beans. Bring a saucepan three-fourths full of water to a boil and add the favas. Boil for 1 minute, then drain. Pinch off the ends and squeeze each bean free of its tough outer skin. If the beans are very small, they may be left unskinned. Set aside.

❀ Refill the saucepan three-fourths full with lightly salted water and bring to a boil. Add the carrots, boil for 2 minutes, and scoop out with a slotted spoon. Immerse immediately in ice water to stop the cooking, then scoop out and set aside. Repeat with the asparagus, blanching for 1 minute, and the snap peas, blanching for 30 seconds.

❀ Bring a large pot three-fourths full of salted water to a rolling boil. Add the pasta, stir well, and cook until al dente (tender but firm to the bite), 3–4 minutes or according to package directions. Drain and transfer to a warmed bowl. Toss with 3 tablespoons of the olive oil. Keep warm.

❀ While the water is heating for the pasta, in a sauté pan over medium heat, warm the remaining 3 tablespoons olive oil. Add the onion and sauté until golden brown, 5–7 minutes. Add the stock and bring to a boil. Boil until reduced by one-half, 10–15 minutes. Add the carrots, asparagus, peas, and the fava beans. Heat until the vegetables are warmed through and just tender, 3–4 minutes. Season with salt and pepper.

❀ Toss the vegetable mixture with the pasta, turn into a warmed serving bowl, and scatter the tomatoes and basil on top. Sprinkle with the Parmesan and serve at once.

NUTRITIONAL ANALYSIS PER SERVING: Calories 560 (Kilojoules 2,352); Protein 19 g; Carbohydrates 74 g; Total Fat 21 g; Saturated Fat 4 g; Cholesterol 6 mg; Sodium 198 mg; Dietary Fiber 5 g

Pizzettas with Spring Herb Pesto

PREP TIME: 40 MINUTES, PLUS
1¼ HOURS FOR RISING

COOKING TIME: 30 MINUTES

INGREDIENTS

FOR THE DOUGH

I package (2½ teaspoons) active dry
yeast

2 tablespoons sugar

1½ cups (12 fl oz/375 ml) lukewarm
water (105–115°F/40–46°C)

3½ cups (17½ oz/545 g) all-purpose
(plain) flour

½ cup (2½ oz/75 g) semolina flour

I tablespoon salt

2 teaspoons minced fresh rosemary

3 tablespoons olive oil

FOR THE PESTO

¼ cup (1¼ oz/37 g) slivered blanched
almonds

I clove garlic

¼ cup (¼ oz/7 g) each fresh chervil
leaves and flat-leaf (Italian) parsley

½ teaspoon minced fresh rosemary

¼ cup (¼ oz/7 g) snipped fresh garlic
chives or regular chives

¼ cup (2 fl oz/60 ml) extra-virgin
olive oil

¼ cup (1 oz/30 g) grated Parmesan
cheese

¼ lb (125 g) part-skim mozzarella
cheese, shredded

3 tomatoes, thinly sliced

To store the leftover pesto, transfer to a small jar, float a film of
olive oil on top, and cap tightly. Refrigerate for up to 2 months.

MAKES EIGHT 6-INCH (15-CM) PIZZAS; SERVES 4

❊ To make the dough, in a small bowl, dissolve the yeast and sugar in
the lukewarm water; let stand until bubbles rise, about 5 minutes.

❊ In a large bowl, combine the all-purpose flour, semolina flour, salt,
and rosemary. Stir in the yeast mixture and olive oil until a dough forms.
Turn out the dough onto a lightly floured work surface and knead by
hand until smooth, satiny, and no longer sticky, 5–8 minutes, adding
more flour or water as necessary. Form into a ball and place in a lightly
oiled bowl, turning to grease all sides. Cover with plastic wrap and let
rise for 30 minutes.

❊ Turn out the dough onto the lightly floured work surface and press
flat. Divide into 8 equal portions. Form each portion into a ball. Lightly
oil a baking sheet and place the balls on it. Cover with plastic wrap and
let rise until almost doubled in bulk, about 45 minutes.

❊ Meanwhile, make the pesto: Preheat an oven to 350°F (180°C). Spread
the almonds on a baking sheet and toast until lightly browned, 5–7 minutes. Let cool. Raise the temperature to 450°F (230°C). Place a pizza
stone in the oven to preheat or oil another baking sheet.

❊ With a food processor running, drop in the garlic clove. Then add the
chervil, parsley, rosemary, chives, and almonds and process to a grainy
texture. Again with the food processor running, add the olive oil in a
slow stream until combined. Pour into a bowl and fold in the Parmesan.
You should have about ½ cup (4 fl oz/125 ml). Set aside.

❊ On the lightly floured work surface, roll out each ball of dough into
a round 6 inches (15 cm) in diameter. Leaving a ½-inch (12-mm) border,
spread 1 teaspoon of the pesto over each round. Sprinkle a little mozzarella cheese over each round, then arrange the tomato slices on top.

❊ Baking in 2 batches, transfer the pizzettas to the prepared baking
sheet or pizza stone and bake until the dough is lightly browned and the
cheese is melted, about 10 minutes. Serve at once.

NUTRITIONAL ANALYSIS PER SERVING: Calories 940 (Kilojoules 3,948); Protein 28 g;
Carbohydrates 122 g; Total Fat 38 g; Saturated Fat 8 g; Cholesterol 21 mg; Sodium 1,902 mg;
Dietary Fiber 6 g

Brown Rice and Broccoli Rabe Pilaf

PREP TIME: 15 MINUTES

COOKING TIME: 1 HOUR

INGREDIENTS

3 tablespoons vegetable oil

2 shallots, minced

1½ cups (10½ oz/330 g) Wehani brown rice

3 cups (24 fl oz/750 ml) Vegetable Stock (*page 9*), heated

½ lb (250 g) broccoli rabe (*see note*), trimmed and coarsely chopped

salt and ground pepper to taste

¾ cup (4 oz/125 g) chopped cashews

¼ cup (1 oz/30 g) grated Parmesan cheese

1 teaspoon minced fresh flat-leaf (Italian) parsley

PREP TIP: Wehani brown rice is a variety of basmati rice grown in the United States. It has a mahogany-colored bran and is aromatic and nutty tasting. Look for it in health-food stores.

You can find the broccoli rabe for this robust main course in produce markets from autumn to spring. When it is not available, use broccoli florets instead. White rice can be substituted, but it will cook in only 20 minutes; add the broccoli rabe for the final 10 minutes of cooking.

SERVES 6

❈ In a large saucepan over medium heat, warm the vegetable oil. Add the shallots and sauté until softened, 3–4 minutes. Stir in the rice and cook, stirring constantly, until the rice is lightly browned, 3–4 minutes. Add the stock and reduce the heat to low. Cover and cook, stirring occasionally, for 30 minutes.

❈ Stir in the broccoli rabe and continue to cook until the rice is tender, 10–15 minutes longer. Season with salt and pepper, then remove from the heat.

❈ Preheat a broiler (griller). Lightly oil a flameproof 9-by-13-inch (23-by-33-cm) baking dish.

❈ In a small bowl, combine the cashews, Parmesan cheese, and parsley. Transfer the rice mixture to the prepared baking dish. Sprinkle the cashew mixture evenly over the top. Place under the broiler about 3 inches (7.5 cm) below the heat source and broil (grill) until golden brown, 3–4 minutes.

❈ Remove from the broiler and serve at once.

NUTRITIONAL ANALYSIS PER SERVING: Calories 410 (Kilojoules 1,722); Protein 10 g; Carbohydrates 46 g; Total Fat 22 g; Saturated Fat 4 g; Cholesterol 4 mg; Sodium 102 mg; Dietary Fiber 3 g

Barley and Root Vegetable Stew

PREP TIME: 25 MINUTES

COOKING TIME: 1¼ HOURS

INGREDIENTS

6 tablespoons (3 fl oz/90 ml) extra-virgin olive oil

1 yellow onion, finely chopped

1 carrot, peeled and finely chopped

1 celery stalk, finely chopped

1 cup (8 fl oz/250 ml) dry white wine

5½ cups (44 fl oz/1.3 l) Vegetable Stock (page 9)

½ cup (4 oz/125 g) pearl barley

¼ cup (⅓ oz/10 g) minced fresh flat-leaf (Italian) parsley

2 teaspoons minced fresh thyme

1 celery root (celeriac), peeled and diced

½ lb (250 g) Jerusalem artichokes, peeled and quartered (see note)

3 parsnips, peeled and thinly sliced crosswise

1 red (Spanish) onion, cut into 1-inch (2.5-cm) pieces

1 potato, unpeeled, cut into 1-inch (2.5-cm) pieces

2 teaspoons coarse sea salt

salt and ground pepper to taste

This winter stew is a powerhouse of energy, fueled by a healthy measure of carbohydrates. Jerusalem artichokes, sometimes called sunchokes, are also an excellent source of iron. If you have trouble finding them, add an additional potato or another favorite root vegetable in their place.

SERVES 6

❈ Preheat an oven to 400°F (200°C). Lightly oil a baking sheet.

❈ In a large, heavy saucepan over medium-high heat, warm 3 tablespoons of the olive oil. Add the yellow onion, carrot, and celery and sauté until browned, 7–8 minutes. Raise the heat to high, add the wine, and deglaze the pan, stirring with a wooden spoon to dislodge any browned bits from the pan bottom. Continue to cook until the wine is reduced by one-half, about 5 minutes.

❈ Add the stock and bring to a boil over high heat. Add the barley, parsley, and thyme and reduce the heat to medium-low. Cook, uncovered, for 35 minutes. Add the celery root, Jerusalem artichokes, and parsnips. Cover and cook over medium-low heat until tender, 15–20 minutes longer.

❈ Meanwhile, in a large bowl, combine the red onion, potato, and the remaining 3 tablespoons olive oil. Toss to coat well. Spread on the prepared baking sheet and sprinkle with the sea salt. Roast until the vegetables are browned and tender, 40–45 minutes.

❈ Add the roasted vegetables to the stockpot and stir well. Season with salt and pepper.

❈ Ladle into warmed bowls to serve.

NUTRITIONAL ANALYSIS PER SERVING: Calories 387 (Kilojoules 1,625); Protein 6 g; Carbohydrates 51 g; Total Fat 20 g; Saturated Fat 3 g; Cholesterol 0 mg; Sodium 589 mg; Dietary Fiber 8 g

Green Garlic, Baby Bok Choy, and Baby Corn in Orange-Tamarind Sauce

PREP TIME: 20 MINUTES, PLUS
30 MINUTES FOR SOAKING

COOKING TIME: 30 MINUTES,
PLUS 30 MINUTES FOR
SOAKING

INGREDIENTS

2 cups (16 fl oz/500 ml) fresh orange juice

2 cups (16 fl oz/500 ml) Vegetable Stock (page 9)

2 tablespoons tamarind pulp, broken into small pieces

1 tablespoon sugar

1 clove garlic, minced

½ teaspoon peeled and minced fresh ginger

½ teaspoon chile paste, or to taste

6 heads green garlic (see note)

12 ears of baby corn, fresh or canned, or 1½ cups (9 oz/280 g) corn kernels

ice water as needed

3 tablespoons peanut oil

1 lb (500 g) baby bok choy (see note), trimmed, sliced crosswise, and stems and leaves separated

about ¼ lb (125 g) dried bean thread noodles, soaked in warm water for 30 minutes

The pulp of the tamarind, a bittersweet pod fruit, is sold in small, compressed blocks in Asian, Indian, and South American markets. Springtime brings immature green garlic to farmers' markets, ready for you to use in this bright-tasting stir-fry. If unavailable, substitute 1 clove garlic, minced, for each head. Spinach can be substituted for the bok choy.

SERVES 4

❋ In a saucepan over high heat, combine the orange juice and stock. Bring to a boil and boil until reduced by one-half, about 10 minutes. Remove from the heat and add the tamarind. Then stir in the sugar until dissolved. Let stand for 30 minutes. Using a fork, mash the tamarind and strain through a fine-mesh sieve into a bowl, pressing to extract as much liquid as possible. Add the garlic, ginger, and chile paste. Set aside.

❋ Trim off the root end and all but 2 inches (5 cm) of the green tops from each head of green garlic. Mince the remaining green tops and set aside. Quarter each garlic head lengthwise. If using fresh baby corn, bring a saucepan three-fourths full of water to a boil. Remove the husks and silks and add the baby corn to the boiling water. Blanch for 30 seconds and drain. Immerse in ice water and drain again. Set aside.

❋ In a wok or large sauté pan over high heat, warm the peanut oil until very hot but not smoking. Add the minced garlic tops and quartered heads and toss and stir for 1 minute. Add the bok choy stems and baby corn or corn kernels and toss and stir for 1 minute longer. Stir in the tamarind mixture, reduce the heat to medium, and simmer until the flavors are blended, about 10 minutes. Add the bok choy leaves and continue to cook, stirring occasionally, until the garlic is tender, 5–8 minutes longer.

❋ Meanwhile, drain the noodles and cut into 6-inch (15-cm) lengths. Add to the pan and toss and stir until heated through. Transfer to a warmed serving bowl and serve immediately.

NUTRITIONAL ANALYSIS PER SERVING: Calories 363 (Kilojoules 1,525); Protein 5 g; Carbohydrates 59 g; Total Fat 14 g; Saturated Fat 2 g; Cholesterol 0 mg; Sodium 109 mg; Dietary Fiber 4 g

Leek, Artichoke, and Chard Tart

PREP TIME: 35 MINUTES, PLUS
1 HOUR FOR CHILLING

COOKING TIME: 1¼ HOURS,
PLUS 15 MINUTES FOR
COOLING

INGREDIENTS

FOR THE PASTRY

1¼ cups (6½ oz/200 g) all-purpose (plain) flour

½ teaspoon salt

½ cup (4 oz/125 g) chilled unsalted butter, cut into tablespoon-sized pieces

4–5 tablespoons (2–3 fl oz/60–80 ml) ice water

FOR THE FILLING

juice of 1 lemon

2 artichokes

3 tablespoons olive oil

2 leeks, white part only, thinly sliced crosswise

1 cup (8 fl oz/250 ml) Rich Vegetable Stock (page 9)

2 cups (4 oz/125 g) shredded red Swiss chard leaves

salt and ground pepper to taste

1 cup (8 fl oz/250 ml) milk

2 eggs

1 teaspoon ground coriander

¼ cup (1 oz/30 g) fine dried bread crumbs mixed with 1 teaspoon minced fresh parsley

¼ lb (125 g) fresh goat cheese, crumbled

Artichokes are harvested in spring and autumn. Choose dense ones with tightly closed leaves.

MAKES ONE 10-INCH (25-CM) TART; SERVES 8

❊ To make the pastry, in a food processor, combine the flour and salt. Process to mix. With the machine running, drop in the butter pieces, one at a time, and process until evenly distributed. Using on-off pulses, add only as much of the ice water as needed for the dough to begin to hold together. Form into a ball, flatten into a disk, and wrap in plastic wrap. Refrigerate for at least 1 hour or for up to 12 hours.

❊ Preheat an oven to 350°F (180°C). On a lightly floured work surface, roll out the dough into a round 12 inches (30 cm) in diameter. Carefully transfer to a 10-inch (25-cm) tart pan with a removable bottom and trim even with the pan rim. Line with parchment (baking) paper and fill with pie weights. Bake until firm and lightly colored, about 15 minutes. Remove the weights and paper and let cool slightly.

❊ Meanwhile, make the filling: Fill a bowl three-fourths full with water and add the lemon juice. Cut off the stem from each artichoke, then cut off the top third. Break off all the tough outer leaves until you reach the tender, pale inner leaves. Trim away the tough layer on the base. Drop the artichokes into the lemon water as they are trimmed. Bring a saucepan three-fourths full of water to a boil. Drain the artichokes, add to the pan, and cook until tender, 12–15 minutes. Drain, cool slightly, and scrape out the chokes. Chop the artichokes; you should have about 1 cup (6 oz/185 g).

❊ In a large sauté pan over medium heat, warm the olive oil. Add the leeks and sauté until softened, 4–5 minutes. Add the stock, bring to a boil, and add the artichokes and chard. Cover and cook until the chard is wilted, 3–5 minutes. Season with salt and pepper. Let cool. In a bowl, beat together the milk, eggs, and coriander. Stir into the cooled vegetable mixture. Pour into the prebaked shell.

❊ Bake until the filling is partially set, about 20 minutes. Sprinkle with the bread crumbs, and dot with the cheese. Continue baking until a knife inserted into the center comes out clean, 10–15 minutes. Let stand for 15 minutes, then serve warm.

NUTRITIONAL ANALYSIS PER SERVING: Calories 358 (Kilojoules 1504); Protein 9 g; Carbohydrates 29 g; Total Fat 23 g; Saturated Fat 11 g; Cholesterol 95 mg; Sodium 334 mg; Dietary Fiber 1 g

Stuffed Anaheim Chiles with Creamy Guacamole Sauce

PREP TIME: 30 MINUTES

COOKING TIME: 50 MINUTES

INGREDIENTS

FOR THE GUACAMOLE SAUCE

2 ripe avocados, pitted and peeled

½ cup (4 fl oz/125 ml) sour cream

½ cup (4 fl oz/125 ml) Vegetable
Stock (page 9)

1 teaspoon grated lemon zest

salt and ground pepper to taste

red pepper flakes to taste

FOR THE CHILES

8 Anaheim chiles

3 tablespoons olive oil

1 red (Spanish) onion, minced

3 cloves garlic, minced

1¼ cups (10 fl oz/310 ml) Vegetable
Stock (page 9)

½ cup (3½ oz/105 g) medium-grain
white rice

2 plum (Roma) tomatoes, peeled,
seeded, and diced (see technique,
page 13)

2 tablespoons minced fresh cilantro
(fresh coriander)

½ cup (2 oz/60 g) shredded cheddar
cheese

salt and ground pepper to taste

The guacamole sauce in this lively summertime main course is an elegant variation on the famed dip found in Mexican restaurants on both sides of the border. The Anaheim chiles are mild; if you prefer a slightly spicier dish, use poblanos and sprinkle a little chili powder on top before serving.

SERVES 4

❀ To make the sauce, in a blender or food processor, combine the avocados, sour cream, stock, and lemon zest. Process until smooth. Transfer to a bowl and season with salt, pepper, and red pepper flakes. Set aside.

❀ Preheat a broiler (griller). Place the chiles on a baking sheet. Broil (grill), turning as needed, until the skins blacken and blister. Remove from the broiler, drape the peppers loosely with aluminum foil, and let cool for 10 minutes, then peel away the skins. Make a lengthwise slit in each chile and carefully remove the seeds. Leave the stems intact and try to maintain the shape of the chiles. Set the chiles aside.

❀ Preheat an oven to 375°F (190°C). Lightly oil a baking sheet.

❀ To make the filling, in a sauté pan over medium heat, warm the olive oil. Add the onion and garlic and sauté until softened, about 3 minutes. Raise the heat to medium-high, pour in the stock, and deglaze the pan, stirring with a wooden spoon to dislodge any browned bits from the pan bottom. Add the rice, reduce the heat to low, and simmer until the liquid is absorbed, 10–15 minutes. Stir in the tomatoes and cilantro and heat through. Add the cheese and season with salt and pepper. Remove from the heat.

❀ Spoon the filling into the chiles, packing them well and keeping their shape. Place on the prepared baking sheet, slit sides up, cover with aluminum foil, and bake until the cheese is melted, about 20 minutes.

❀ To serve, transfer the chiles to warmed individual plates, allowing 2 chiles for each serving. Pass the guacamole sauce at the table.

NUTRITIONAL ANALYSIS PER SERVING: Calories 554 (Kilojoules 2,327); Protein 11 g; Carbohydrates 44 g; Total Fat 40 g; Saturated Fat 11 g; Cholesterol 28 mg; Sodium 131 mg; Dietary Fiber 5 g

Butternut Squash Risotto

PREP TIME: 20 MINUTES

COOKING TIME: 1 HOUR

INGREDIENTS

1 lb (500 g) butternut squash

7½–8 cups (60–64 fl oz/1.9–2 l)
Vegetable Stock (page 9)

2 tablespoons minced fresh flat-leaf
(Italian) parsley, plus chopped
parsley for garnish

¼ teaspoon ground nutmeg

salt and ground pepper to taste

¼ cup (2 fl oz/60 ml) extra-virgin
olive oil

1 yellow onion, diced

1½ cups (10½ oz/330 g) Carnaroli or
Arborio rice

PREP TIP: You'll find medium-grain
Italian rice varieties for risotto such
as Arborio, Carnaroli, or Vialone
Nano in Italian delicatessens,
specialty-food stores, and well-
stocked markets.

This risotto, made with Italian medium-grain rice, is packed into individual ramekins and unmolded onto small mounds of butternut squash purée. Accompanied by a salad, it makes a memorable harvesttime or holiday luncheon.

SERVES 6

❀ Preheat an oven to 375°F (190°C). Line a baking sheet with parchment (baking) paper.

❀ Cut the butternut squash in half through the stem end and scoop out and discard the seeds and fibers. Place the squash halves, cut sides down, on the prepared baking sheet. Bake until softened, 20–25 minutes. Transfer to a rack and let cool.

❀ Pour the stock into a saucepan and bring to a boil. Reduce the heat to low so that the stock barely simmers.

❀ Scoop out the pulp from the cooled squash halves and place in a food processor with ¼ cup (2 fl oz/60 ml) of the stock. Purée until smooth. Transfer to a saucepan and add the parsley and nutmeg. Season with salt and pepper. Cover to keep warm, adding a little stock if the purée begins to dry out.

❀ In a saucepan over medium heat, warm the olive oil. Add the onion and sauté until softened, about 3 minutes. Add the rice, stir to coat with the oil, and cook, stirring, until the edges are translucent, 3–4 minutes. Add a ladleful of the simmering stock and continue to stir constantly over medium heat. When the stock is almost fully absorbed, add another ladleful. Stir steadily to keep the rice from sticking and continue to add more stock, a ladleful at a time, as soon as each ladleful is almost absorbed. The risotto is done when the rice is tender but firm, about 20 minutes total. Stir in ¼ cup (2 oz/60 g) of the squash purée and season with salt and pepper.

❀ Divide the remaining squash purée among 6 individual plates. Working quickly, spoon about 1 cup of the risotto into a 1-cup (8–fl oz/250-ml) ramekin, packing it tightly. Unmold the risotto on top of the squash purée. Repeat with the remaining risotto to make 6 servings. Garnish with chopped parsley and serve.

NUTRITIONAL ANALYSIS PER SERVING: Calories 392 (Kilojoules 1,646); Protein 6 g; Carbohydrates 59 g; Total Fat 16 g; Saturated Fat 2 g; Cholesterol 0 mg; Sodium 13 mg; Dietary Fiber 2 g

Vegetarian Cassoulet

PREP TIME: 25 MINUTES, PLUS
3 HOURS FOR SOAKING

COOKING TIME: 2 HOURS

INGREDIENTS

1 cup (7 oz/220 g) dried small white beans

6 tablespoons (3 fl oz/90 ml) extra-virgin olive oil

1 yellow onion, chopped

1 carrot, peeled and chopped

1 celery stalk, chopped, leaves reserved

4 cups (32 fl oz/1 l) Vegetable Stock (page 9)

1 fresh thyme sprig, plus 1 teaspoon minced fresh thyme

1 fresh flat-leaf (Italian) parsley sprig

1 bay leaf

2 cloves garlic, minced, plus 10 whole cloves garlic

1 lb (500 g) red potatoes, unpeeled and cut into 2-inch (5-cm) chunks

1 red (Spanish) onion, cut into 1-inch (2.5-cm) chunks

1 tablespoon coarse sea salt

½ lb (250 g) fresh portobello mushrooms, brushed clean and stems and gills removed, cut into 2-inch (5-cm) chunks

1 cup (8 fl oz/250 ml) dry white wine

½ cup (2½ oz/75 g) well-drained, oil-packed sun-dried tomatoes

salt and ground pepper to taste

Hearty chunks of oven-roasted vegetables replace the meat that is traditionally found in this robust winter dish.

SERVES 6

❊ Pick over the beans and discard any damaged beans or impurities. Rinse the beans. Place in a bowl, add water to cover generously, and let soak for about 3 hours.

❊ In a saucepan over medium heat, warm 3 tablespoons of the olive oil. Add the onion, carrot, and chopped celery and sauté until lightly browned, 5–7 minutes. Add the stock, raise the heat to high, and bring to a boil. Drain the beans and add them to the pan. Gather the thyme sprig, parsley sprig, bay leaf, and celery leaves into a bundle and tie securely with kitchen string. Add to the pan along with the minced garlic. Reduce the heat to low, cover, and simmer until the beans are tender, about 1½ hours. Discard the herb bundle.

❊ Meanwhile, preheat an oven to 400°F (200°C). Lightly oil a large flameproof baking dish. In a large bowl, combine the potatoes, red onion, and the remaining 3 tablespoons olive oil. Toss to coat well. Spread in the prepared baking dish and sprinkle with the sea salt.

❊ Roast in the oven until lightly browned, about 45 minutes. Add the mushrooms and whole garlic cloves and continue to roast until the vegetables are browned, about 15 minutes longer.

❊ Remove from the oven, transfer the vegetables to a plate, and set aside. Place the baking dish on the stove top over medium heat. Pour in the white wine and deglaze the dish, stirring with a wooden spoon to dislodge any browned bits from the dish bottom. Continue to cook until the wine is almost evaporated, 5–7 minutes. Add the cooked beans and their liquid, the roasted vegetables, minced thyme, and sun-dried tomatoes. Season with salt and pepper. Continue to cook until the vegetables are tender, 15–20 minutes. Serve at once.

NUTRITIONAL ANALYSIS PER SERVING: Calories 417 (Kilojoules 1,751); Protein 12 g; Carbohydrates 50 g; Total Fat 21 g; Saturated Fat 3 g; Cholesterol 0 mg; Sodium 833 mg; Dietary Fiber 8 g

Rutabaga, Squash, and Mushroom Ragout

PREP TIME: 25 MINUTES

COOKING TIME: 1 HOUR

INGREDIENTS

3 tablespoons extra-virgin olive oil

1 large red (Spanish) onion, diced

2 cups (16 fl oz/500 ml) Vegetable
Stock *(page 9)*

1 cup (8 fl oz/250 ml) carrot juice

2 rutabagas (swedes), peeled and
finely diced

1 Table Queen squash or other
winter squash *(see note)*, about
1 lb (500 g), peeled, seeded, and
finely diced

1 butternut squash, about 1 lb
(500 g), peeled and finely diced

1 lb (500 g) fresh button mushrooms,
brushed clean and stemmed

1 cup (6 oz/185 g) pitted prunes,
coarsely chopped

½ teaspoon dried thyme

½ teaspoon dried marjoram

salt and ground pepper to taste

2 tablespoons minced fresh flat-leaf
(Italian) parsley

A ragout is simply a well-seasoned stew, usually with a thick sauce. Simmered slowly to bring out deep, rich flavors, this autumn dish is at once satisfying and healthy. Try using other squash varieties such as spaghetti squash, Hubbard squash, or sugar pumpkin. Serve this rich combination over couscous, bulgur, or steamed brown rice.

SERVES 6

✽ In a heavy saucepan over medium heat, warm the olive oil. Add the onion and sauté until softened, about 5 minutes. Add the stock and carrot juice, raise the heat to high, and bring to a boil. Add the rutabagas and squashes, reduce the heat to medium-low, and simmer, uncovered, for 30 minutes.

✽ Add the mushrooms, prunes, thyme, and marjoram and continue to cook until all the vegetables are tender, 15–20 minutes longer. Season with salt and pepper. Ladle into warmed bowls and sprinkle with the parsley. Serve at once.

NUTRITIONAL ANALYSIS PER SERVING: Calories 263 (Kilojoules 1,105); Protein 6 g; Carbohydrates 46 g; Total Fat 9 g; Saturated Fat 1 g; Cholesterol 0 mg; Sodium 38 mg; Dietary Fiber 7 g

Herbed Mushroom and Chestnut Crepes

PREP TIME: 40 MINUTES, PLUS
1 HOUR FOR CHILLING

COOKING TIME: 35 MINUTES

INGREDIENTS

FOR THE CREPES

1 cup (5 oz/155 g) all-purpose (plain) flour

1 cup (8 fl oz/250 ml) Rich Vegetable Stock *(page 9)*

3 eggs

2 tablespoons unsalted butter, melted, plus melted butter for cooking

3 tablespoons finely snipped fresh chives

2 teaspoons minced fresh thyme

FOR THE FILLING

1 lb (500 g) chestnuts

3 tablespoons olive oil

4 green (spring) onions, thinly sliced

1 lb (500 g) fresh mushrooms, brushed clean, stemmed, and thinly sliced

1 cup (7 oz/220 g) cooked brown rice *(page 15)*

1 tablespoon minced fresh flat-leaf (Italian) parsley

1 teaspoon minced fresh marjoram

salt and ground pepper to taste

Serve these crepes as part of an elegant fall dinner. Look for fresh chestnuts in autumn and throughout the holiday season. If they cannot be found, substitute ¾ pound (375 g) canned chestnuts. If desired, garnish with any of the herbs featured in the recipe.

MAKES 16 FILLED CREPES; SERVES 6

❋ To make the crepe batter, combine the flour, stock, eggs, and 2 tablespoons melted butter in a blender or food processor. Process until smooth. Transfer to a bowl and stir in the chives and thyme. Cover and chill for at least 1 hour or for up to 12 hours.

❋ Meanwhile, to roast the chestnuts, preheat an oven to 450°F (230°C). Using a sharp knife, score an X in the shell on the flat side of each chestnut, then place in a baking pan large enough to hold them in a single layer. Add water to the pan to form a very shallow pool in the bottom. Bake until the shells begin to turn brittle and peel back at the Xs, 10–20 minutes. Remove from the oven and, while the nuts are still warm, peel off the brittle shells and the furry skin directly beneath them. Coarsely chop the nuts.

❋ Place an 8-inch (20-cm) nonstick frying pan over medium heat. When the pan is hot, brush with melted butter. Stir the batter and pour ¼ cup (2 fl oz/60 ml) of it into the pan. Tilt the pan to create a thin, even layer of batter. Immediately loosen the edges with a spatula and cook until the top is set and looks dry, about 1 minute. Turn and cook just to brown lightly on the second side, 15–30 seconds longer. Transfer to a plate and repeat with the remaining batter. Stack the crepes between sheets of parchment (baking) paper or waxed paper as they are cooked. You should have 16 crepes in all.

❋ In a sauté pan over medium heat, warm the olive oil. Add the green onions and sauté until softened, 2–3 minutes. Add the chestnuts and mushrooms and cook, stirring occasionally, until most of the mushroom liquid has evaporated, 8–10 minutes. Add the cooked rice, parsley, and marjoram and heat through. Season with salt and pepper.

❋ To assemble, spread 3 tablespoons of the filling evenly on one-half of each crepe. Fold the crepe in half, and then fold in half again. Place on a warmed serving platter and serve at once.

NUTRITIONAL ANALYSIS PER SERVING: Calories 440 (Kilojoules 1,848); Protein 9 g; Carbohydrates 57 g; Total Fat 20 g; Saturated Fat 7 g; Cholesterol 127 mg; Sodium 42 mg; Dietary Fiber 3 g

Cold Soba Noodles with Green Onions and Baby Vegetables

PREP TIME: 20 MINUTES, PLUS
1 HOUR FOR CHILLING

COOKING TIME: 10 MINUTES

INGREDIENTS

½ lb (250 g) dried soba noodles

4 cups (32 fl oz/1 l) Rich Vegetable Stock (page 9)

4 ears of baby corn, husks and silks removed and halved lengthwise, or ½ cup (3 oz/90 g) fresh corn kernels

ice water as needed

8 baby zucchini (courgettes), thinly sliced crosswise

1 carrot, peeled and julienned

½ oz (15 g) konbu, finely shredded

¼ cup (2 fl oz/60 ml) soy sauce

2 tablespoons sweet cooking sake such as mirin, or 2 teaspoons sugar

3 green (spring) onions, including tender green tops, thinly sliced

1 sheet nori

PREP TIP: Soba noodles are sold in most well-stocked food markets. The other ingredients called for here may require a trip to a Japanese market. Konbu, or dried kelp, can be stored for 6 months in an airtight container. Nori, the dried seaweed used for sushi, can be kept the same way. Look for toasted nori if you don't have a gas range to toast your own.

The Japanese are especially fond of cold noodle dishes such as this one. Served as a quick lunch, it's a great way to beat the summertime heat.

SERVES 4

✿ Bring a saucepan three-fourths full of water to a boil. Add the soba noodles and cook until tender, 3–5 minutes. Drain and rinse with cold running water. Drain again, cover, and chill well, about 1 hour.

✿ In a saucepan over high heat, bring the stock to a boil. Add the corn and blanch for 1 minute. Scoop out with a slotted spoon and immerse immediately in ice water to stop the cooking. Scoop out of the ice water and set aside. Repeat with the zucchini and carrot. Chill the vegetables separately, about 1 hour.

✿ Meanwhile, remove the stock from the heat and add the konbu, soy sauce, and cooking sake or sugar. Let stand for 30 minutes, then cover and chill well, about 30 minutes.

✿ To serve, ladle the chilled stock mixture into individual bowls, dividing it evenly. Add the soba noodles to the bowls, again dividing evenly, and garnish with the corn, zucchini, carrot, and green onions.

✿ Using tongs, pass the nori over an open flame, turning each side toward the flame 2 or 3 times until toasted. Cut into thin strips or crumble, then sprinkle over the noodles. Serve at once.

NUTRITIONAL ANALYSIS PER SERVING: Calories 341 (Kilojoules 1,432); Protein 12 g; Carbohydrates 60 g; Total Fat 8 g; Saturated Fat 1 g; Cholesterol 0 mg; Sodium 1,596 mg; Dietary Fiber 5 g

Chickpea Stew

PREP TIME: 20 MINUTES, PLUS
3 HOURS FOR SOAKING

COOKING TIME: 2¼ HOURS

INGREDIENTS

¾ cup (5 oz/155 g) dried chickpeas
(garbanzo beans)

5 cups (40 fl oz/1.25 l) Vegetable
Stock (page 9)

1 lb (500 g) baking potatoes, peeled
and diced

1 lb (500 g) tomatoes, peeled and
chopped (see technique, page 13)

2 teaspoons garam masala (see note,
page 31)

½ teaspoon ground ginger

½ teaspoon ground turmeric

salt and ground pepper to taste

3 tablespoons chopped fresh cilantro
(fresh coriander)

COOKING TIP: To save time, substitute 1 can (15 oz/470 g) chickpeas, drained and well rinsed, for the dried ones. Decrease the stock to 3 cups (24 fl oz/750 ml).

Wonderfully seasoned but not too spicy, this cold-weather stew provides an excellent source of protein in its chickpeas. For complete protein, serve it with steamed rice.

SERVES 6

❀ Pick over the chickpeas and discard any damaged beans or impurities. Rinse the chickpeas. Place in a bowl and add water to cover generously. Let soak for 3 hours. Drain.

❀ In a saucepan over high heat, bring the stock to a boil. Add the chickpeas, reduce the heat to medium, and simmer, uncovered, until almost tender, about 1½ hours. Add the potatoes, tomatoes, garam masala, ginger, and turmeric and continue to cook until the chickpeas and potatoes are tender, about 30 minutes longer.

❀ Remove from the heat and let cool slightly. Transfer half of the stock and vegetables to a blender or food processor and purée until smooth. Return to the saucepan and season with salt and pepper. Reheat to serving temperature.

❀ Ladle into warmed bowls, sprinkle with the cilantro, and serve hot.

NUTRITIONAL ANALYSIS PER SERVING: Calories 183 (Kilojoules 769); Protein 6 g; Carbohydrates 29 g; Total Fat 6 g; Saturated Fat 1 g; Cholesterol 0 mg; Sodium 19 mg; Dietary Fiber 3 g

Tofu and Mixed Vegetable Curry

PREP TIME: 15 MINUTES

COOKING TIME: 20 MINUTES

INGREDIENTS

3 tablespoons vegetable oil

2 yellow onions, sliced

I carrot, peeled and grated

2 cloves garlic, minced

2 cups (16 fl oz/500 ml) coconut milk

2 tablespoons curry powder

2 cups (4 oz/125 g) broccoli florets

I cup (2 oz/60 g) cauliflower florets

6 oz (185 g) pressed tofu, cut into
½-inch (12-mm) cubes

salt to taste

PREP TIP: Pressed tofu has been
weighted to remove some of its
moisture. Denser than conventional
tofu, it holds up well in stir-fries
because it is less fragile. Look for
pressed tofu in Japanese stores and
well-stocked food markets, or use
firm tofu instead.

This dish is proof that even in winter months, when produce stalls seem at their barest, you can still put an exciting main course on the table with just a few simple ingredients. Serve this fragrant curry over steamed rice, and garnish with toasted shredded coconut, if you like.

SERVES 6

❀ In a large saucepan over medium heat, warm the vegetable oil. Add the onions and sauté until softened, 4–6 minutes. Add the carrot and garlic and sauté until softened, 2–3 minutes longer.

❀ Add the coconut milk and curry powder, raise the heat to medium-high, and bring to a boil. Add the broccoli, cauliflower, and tofu and reduce the heat to medium-low. Simmer, uncovered, until the vegetables are tender, 5–7 minutes. Season with salt.

❀ Transfer to a warmed serving dish and serve at once.

NUTRITIONAL ANALYSIS PER SERVING: Calories 292 (Kilojoules 1,226); Protein 8 g; Carbohydrates 12 g; Total Fat 26 g; Saturated Fat 15 g; Cholesterol 0 mg; Sodium 30 mg; Dietary Fiber 3 g

Crispy Noodle Pancakes with Black Bean Sauce

PREP TIME: 25 MINUTES, PLUS
20 MINUTES FOR SOAKING

COOKING TIME: 40 MINUTES

INGREDIENTS

FOR THE NOODLE PANCAKES

½ lb (250 g) Chinese rice-stick noodles or vermicelli

2 teaspoons Asian sesame oil

3 tablespoons peanut oil

FOR THE BLACK BEAN SAUCE

½ lb (250 g) asparagus, tough ends removed

ice water as needed

4 dried shiitake mushrooms, soaked in ¼ cup (2 fl oz/60 ml) heated Vegetable Stock (page 9) for 20 minutes, then drained and stock reserved

1 tablespoon fermented black beans (see note)

1 tablespoon dry sherry

1 clove garlic, minced

½ teaspoon peeled and minced fresh ginger

2 tablespoons peanut oil

¼ lb (125 g) fresh shiitake mushrooms, brushed clean, stemmed, and julienned

2 green (spring) onions, thinly sliced

½ teaspoon cornstarch (cornflour) mixed with 1 tablespoon soy sauce

1 small carrot, peeled and julienned

Chinese fermented black beans are soybeans that have been cooked, fermented, and soaked in seasoned brine. These powerful flavor enhancers, a standard pantry item in southern China, are available in most Asian markets.

SERVES 4

❀ Preheat an oven to 200°F (95°C). Lightly oil 8 ramekins, each 3½ inches (9 cm) in diameter, or similar flat-bottomed containers.

❀ To make the noodle pancakes, bring a large pot three-fourths full of salted water to a boil. Add the noodles and cook until just tender, 4–5 minutes. Drain, toss with the sesame oil, and divide into 8 equal portions. Firmly press each portion into a prepared ramekin. Let cool.

❀ In a frying pan over medium-high heat, warm the peanut oil. Carefully invert 2 or 3 of the ramekins, easing the noodle rounds into the pan. Fry until golden brown on the first side, 3–4 minutes. Turn and brown on the second side, about 3 minutes longer. Using a slotted spatula, transfer to paper towels to drain briefly. Keep warm.

❀ To make the sauce, bring a large saucepan three-fourths full of water to a boil, add the asparagus, and blanch for 2 minutes. Drain and immediately immerse in ice water. Drain again, cut on the diagonal into 1-inch (2.5-cm) lengths, and set aside.

❀ Stem and finely dice the rehydrated mushrooms and set aside. Strain the stock through a fine-mesh sieve lined with cheesecloth (muslin); set aside. In a small bowl, combine the black beans, sherry, garlic, and ginger; set aside.

❀ In a large sauté pan over medium heat, warm the peanut oil. Add the fresh mushrooms and sauté until softened, 3–4 minutes. Add the rehydrated mushrooms, asparagus, green onions, and strained stock and cook over high heat to reduce the liquid slightly, about 3 minutes. Add the cornstarch mixture to the black bean mixture and stir well. Cook over medium heat, stirring, until thickened, 3–5 minutes.

❀ To serve, place 2 noodle pancakes on each individual plate. Spoon the sauce over the pancakes and sprinkle with the carrot. Serve at once.

NUTRITIONAL ANALYSIS PER SERVING: Calories 521 (Kilojoules 2,188); Protein 6 g; Carbohydrates 77 g; Total Fat 23 g; Saturated Fat 4 g; Cholesterol 0 mg; Sodium 673 mg; Dietary Fiber 7 g

Anasazi Bean Chili in Corn Cups

PREP TIME: 30 MINUTES, PLUS
3 HOURS FOR SOAKING

COOKING TIME: 2 HOURS

INGREDIENTS

1¾ cups (12 oz/375 g) dried Anasazi
   beans *(see note)*

12 large tomatoes

5 tablespoons olive oil

5 celery stalks, diced

3 carrots, peeled and diced

2 large yellow onions, chopped

5 cloves garlic, minced

1 jalapeño chile, seeded and minced

2¼ teaspoons grated orange zest

3 qt (3 l) Vegetable Stock *(page 9)*

FOR THE CORN CUPS

¼ lb (125 g) cream cheese, at room
   temperature

½ cup (4 oz/125 g) unsalted butter,
   at room temperature

1 egg

1⅓ cups (7 oz/220 g) all-purpose
   (plain) flour

⅔ cup (3½ oz/105 g) masa harina

½ teaspoon baking powder

¼ teaspoon salt

1 tablespoon chili powder

1 teaspoon each ground cumin and
   ground coriander

salt and ground pepper to taste

¼ cup (⅓ oz/10 g) minced fresh
   cilantro (fresh coriander)

Anasazi beans are heirloom beans with beautiful spotted skin. Other dried beans will also work in this satisfying, cold-weather stew, with black beans being an especially good substitute. This chili recipe makes a large quantity. To store, let cool, then freeze any remaining chili in an airtight container for up to 3 months.

SERVES 6

❀ Pick over the beans and discard any damaged beans or impurities. Rinse the beans. Place in a bowl and add water to cover generously. Let soak for 3 hours. Drain.

❀ Peel the tomatoes (see technique, page 13) and purée in a blender or food processor. In a stockpot over medium heat, warm the olive oil. Add the celery, carrots, and onions and sauté until softened, 6–8 minutes. Add the garlic, jalapeño chile, orange zest, stock, and drained beans. Bring to a boil, reduce the heat to low, and simmer gently, uncovered, stirring occasionally, until the beans are tender, about 2 hours.

❀ About 30 minutes before the chili is ready, preheat an oven to 325°F (165°C). Lightly oil six 1-cup (8–fl oz/250-ml) ramekins or other individual baking dishes.

❀ To make the corn cups, in a bowl, beat together the cream cheese and butter until creamy. Beat in the egg. In another bowl, stir together the all-purpose flour, masa harina, baking powder, and salt. Fold into the egg mixture, folding just until blended. Do not overmix.

❀ Using your fingers, line the prepared ramekins or individual baking dishes with the mixture, dividing it evenly. Bake until a light golden brown, 18–20 minutes. Remove from the oven and keep warm.

❀ When the chili is ready, add the chili powder, cumin, and coriander and season with salt and pepper.

❀ To serve, place a corn cup on each individual plate. Spoon the chili into the cups and garnish with the cilantro. Serve at once.

NUTRITIONAL ANALYSIS PER SERVING: Calories 468 (Kilojoules 1,966); Protein 13 g; Carbohydrates 54 g; Total Fat 24 g; Saturated Fat 9 g; Cholesterol 49 mg; Sodium 154 mg; Dietary Fiber 9 g

Polenta Lasagna with Gorgonzola Béchamel Sauce

PREP TIME: 20 MINUTES

COOKING TIME: 1½ HOURS

INGREDIENTS

FOR THE VEGETABLE POLENTA

2 tablespoons olive oil

4 cloves garlic, minced

½ lb (250 g) fresh mushrooms, brushed clean and sliced

1 eggplant (aubergine), about ½ lb (250 g), peeled and finely diced

2 tablespoons minced fresh flat-leaf (Italian) parsley

salt and ground black pepper to taste

4½ cups (36 fl oz/1.1 l) Vegetable Stock (page 9)

1½ cups (7½ oz/235 g) polenta

FOR THE BÉCHAMEL SAUCE

½ cup (4 oz/125 g) unsalted butter

6 tablespoons (2 oz/60 g) all-purpose (plain) flour

3 cups (24 fl oz/750 ml) milk, heated

3 oz (90 g) Gorgonzola cheese, crumbled

1 teaspoon minced fresh thyme

salt and ground white pepper to taste

2 tomatoes, peeled and sliced (see technique, page 13)

2 zucchini (courgettes), coarsely grated

The components of this dish can also be prepared and served separately: the vegetable polenta is tasty without a sauce, and the béchamel sauce is good tossed with pasta.

SERVES 8

❀ To make the polenta, preheat an oven to 375°F (190°C). Lightly oil a baking sheet.

❀ In a sauté pan over medium heat, warm the olive oil. Add the garlic and sauté until softened, 2–3 minutes. Add the mushrooms and eggplant and cook, stirring occasionally, until the liquid evaporates, 10–12 minutes. Stir in the parsley, season with salt and black pepper, and set aside.

❀ In a saucepan over high heat, bring the stock to a boil. Slowly add the polenta, stirring constantly. Reduce the heat to medium and continue to cook, stirring constantly, until the polenta pulls away from the pan sides, about 20 minutes. Remove from the heat and stir in the mushroom mixture. Spread the polenta about ½ inch (12 mm) thick on the prepared baking sheet, smoothing the top. Bake until firm and lightly browned, about 15 minutes. Let cool completely on the baking sheet.

❀ To make the sauce, melt the butter in a heavy saucepan over medium heat. Add the flour and cook, stirring constantly, until incorporated, 2–3 minutes. Slowly add the milk, whisking constantly until smooth. Simmer, stirring often, until thickened, about 10 minutes. Add the Gorgonzola and thyme and stir until the cheese melts. Season with salt and white pepper. Remove from the heat.

❀ If you have turned off the oven, preheat it again to 375°F (190°C). Lightly oil a 9-by-13-inch (23-by-33-cm) baking dish. To assemble the lasagna, spoon enough of the sauce into the prepared baking dish to cover the bottom lightly. Cut a piece of polenta to fit the bottom of the dish and place it on the sauce. Arrange half of the tomato slices in a layer on top and then half of the zucchini. Top with half of the remaining sauce. Cover with the remaining polenta, tomato slices, zucchini, and finally the remaining sauce.

❀ Bake until heated through and bubbly, about 30 minutes. Cut into squares and serve hot.

NUTRITIONAL ANALYSIS PER SERVING: Calories 402 (Kilojoules 1,688); Protein 10 g; Carbohydrates 35 g; Total Fat 26 g; Saturated Fat 12 g; Cholesterol 53 mg; Sodium 202 mg; Dietary Fiber 4 g

Grilled Stuffed Portobello Mushrooms on Porcini Couscous

PREP TIME: 20 MINUTES, PLUS
20 MINUTES FOR SOAKING

COOKING TIME: 30 MINUTES,
PLUS PREPARING FIRE

INGREDIENTS

4 fresh portobello mushrooms, each
    3–4 inches (7.5–10 cm) in diameter

3 tablespoons extra-virgin olive oil

1 shallot, minced

½ cup (4 fl oz/125 ml) Vegetable
    Stock (page 9)

1 sweet potato, peeled and coarsely
    grated

½ lb (250 g) spinach leaves, coarsely
    chopped

salt and ground pepper to taste

½ cup (4 oz/125 g) part-skim ricotta
    cheese

¼ cup (4 oz/125 g) dried porcini,
    soaked in 2 cups (16 fl oz/500 ml)
    warm Vegetable Stock (page 9)
    for 20 minutes

1 cup (5 oz/155 g) quick-cooking
    couscous

2 tablespoons minced fresh flat-leaf
    (Italian) parsley

1 teaspoon minced fresh thyme

COOKING TIP: These mushrooms
can also be made in the oven.
Arrange them on a baking sheet
lined with parchment (baking) paper
and bake in a 375°F (190°C) oven for
10–12 minutes.

Portobello mushrooms are available year-round, so you can make this elegant main course in any season.

SERVES 4

❀ Prepare a fire in a grill. Lightly brush the grill rack with olive oil.

❀ Brush the portobello mushrooms clean, then cut off the stems and remove the dark gills. Set the mushroom caps aside.

❀ In a sauté pan over medium heat, warm the olive oil. Add the shallot and sauté until softened, about 3 minutes. Add the stock, raise the heat to high, and bring to a boil. Reduce the heat to medium and add the sweet potato. Cook uncovered, stirring occasionally, until tender, 5–8 minutes. Add the spinach and cook until wilted, 4–5 minutes. Season with salt and pepper. Remove from the heat.

❀ Add the ricotta to the spinach mixture and stir to combine. Spoon into the mushroom caps, dividing it evenly. Place the mushrooms, filled sides up, on the grill rack about 4 inches (10 cm) above the fire and grill until completely heated through, about 10 minutes.

❀ Meanwhile, drain the porcini, reserving the liquid. Chop the porcini. Strain the liquid through a fine-mesh sieve lined with a double thickness of cheesecloth (muslin) into a saucepan. Bring to a boil, add the couscous, parsley, and thyme, and remove from the heat. Cover and let stand for 5 minutes. Uncover and add the porcini. Fluff with a fork and season with salt and pepper. Keep warm until the grilled mushrooms are ready.

❀ Spoon the couscous onto a warmed serving platter and arrange the stuffed mushrooms on top. Serve at once.

NUTRITIONAL ANALYSIS PER SERVING: Calories 381 (Kilojoules 1,600); Protein 13 g; Carbohydrates 48 g; Total Fat 17 g; Saturated Fat 3 g; Cholesterol 9 mg; Sodium 97 mg; Dietary Fiber 6 g

Spinach, Corn, and Potato Enchiladas

PREP TIME: 30 MINUTES

COOKING TIME: 1½ HOURS

INGREDIENTS

2 large baking potatoes

½ cup (3 oz/90 g) corn kernels

1 large red bell pepper (capsicum), seeded and diced

1 yellow onion, coarsely chopped

10 oz (315 g) spinach leaves, thinly sliced

1 can (28 fl oz/875 ml) enchilada sauce

salt and ground pepper to taste

12 corn tortillas

¼ lb (125 g) cheddar cheese, shredded

COOKING TIP: Many enchilada recipes call for frying the tortillas, but in this healthier version they are dipped into the sauce without frying them first. Don't leave the tortillas in the sauce too long, though, or they'll fall apart.

Filling and full of flavor, these enchiladas are at their best made with fresh summer corn, although frozen corn can be used instead.

MAKES 12 ENCHILADAS; SERVES 6

❋ Preheat an oven to 375°F (190°C).

❋ Place the potatoes on a baking sheet and bake until tender when pierced with the tip of a knife, 40–45 minutes. Let cool completely, then dice and set aside.

❋ Reduce the oven temperature to 350°F (180°C).

❋ In a saucepan, combine the potatoes, corn, bell pepper, onion, and spinach. Add 1 cup (8 fl oz/250 ml) of the enchilada sauce and mix well. Place over medium heat, cover tightly, and cook until the spinach is wilted, 5–6 minutes. Remove from the heat, season with salt and pepper, and set aside.

❋ Pour about ½ cup (4 fl oz/125 ml) of the remaining enchilada sauce into a 9-by-13-inch (23-by-33-cm) baking dish. It should just cover the bottom.

❋ In a wide frying pan over medium heat, warm the remaining enchilada sauce. One at a time, dip each tortilla into the warm sauce, allowing it to warm just enough to become pliable. Then, place it in the prepared baking dish, and spoon about one-twelfth of the potato mixture along its center. Roll it up and arrange it in the dish, seam side down. Repeat with remaining tortillas and filling. The dish should be tightly packed.

❋ Pour any sauce remaining in the pan over the enchiladas. Sprinkle with the cheddar cheese.

❋ Bake until heated through and the cheese is melted, 20–25 minutes. Serve directly from the dish.

NUTRITIONAL ANALYSIS PER SERVING: Calories 357 (Kilojoules 1,499); Protein 13 g; Carbohydrates 63 g; Total Fat 8 g; Saturated Fat 4 g; Cholesterol 20 mg; Sodium 1,516 mg; Dietary Fiber 6 g

Escarole Soufflé

PREP TIME: 15 MINUTES

COOKING TIME: 50 MINUTES

INGREDIENTS

1½ tablespoons unsalted butter, melted, plus 2 tablespoons unsalted butter

3 tablespoons finely grated Parmesan cheese

3 tablespoons extra-virgin olive oil

2 leeks, white part only, thinly sliced

2 cups (4 oz/125 g) finely shredded escarole (Batavian endive), *(see note)*

2 tablespoons all-purpose (plain) flour

¾ cup (6 fl oz/180 ml) Vegetable Stock *(page 9)*

¼ teaspoon cayenne pepper

salt and ground black pepper to taste

3 eggs, separated

COOKING TIP: A hot-water bath, or bain-marie, is used to provide moist, even heat for baking delicate egg dishes such as soufflés and custards. Take care when removing the 2 containers from the oven; the water will be dangerously hot.

Escarole, a member of the chicory family, is at its peak in fall and winter. Other bitter greens can be used in its place.

SERVES 6

❀ Preheat an oven to 350°F (180°C). Brush a 1-qt (1-l) soufflé dish with the 1½ tablespoons melted butter. Coat with the Parmesan cheese, tapping out the excess.

❀ In a sauté pan over medium heat, warm the olive oil. Add the leeks and sauté until softened, 5–7 minutes. Add the shredded escarole and sauté until tender, 3–4 minutes longer. Remove from the heat and set aside to cool.

❀ In a saucepan over medium heat, melt the 2 tablespoons butter. Add the flour and cook, stirring, until well incorporated, 3–4 minutes. Slowly add the stock while whisking constantly. Bring to a boil, reduce the heat to low and cook, stirring, until thickened, 5–6 minutes. Add the cayenne pepper, salt, and black pepper. Set aside to cool.

❀ In a large bowl, combine the cooled escarole-leek mixture and the flour-stock mixture. Add the egg yolks and stir with a large spoon to mix well. In a bowl, beat the egg whites until stiff peaks form. Stir about one-third of the whites into the escarole mixture to lighten it. Then fold in the remaining egg whites just until no white streaks remain.

❀ Pour into the prepared soufflé dish and place the dish in a large baking pan. Pour hot water into the baking pan to reach halfway up the sides of the soufflé dish. Bake until the soufflé rises nicely and is lightly browned, about 30 minutes.

NUTRITIONAL ANALYSIS PER SERVING: Calories 213 (Kilojoules 897); Protein 6 g; Carbohydrates 9 g; Total Fat 18 g; Saturated Fat 7 g; Cholesterol 127 mg; Sodium 103 mg; Dietary Fiber 1 g

Cinnamon-Poached Pears with Blood Orange Sauce

PREP TIME: 20 MINUTES

COOKING TIME: 1 HOUR

INGREDIENTS

2 cups (1 lb/500 g) sugar

3 cups (24 fl oz/750 ml) water

1 cinnamon stick

2 teaspoons grated orange zest

5 blood oranges

3 firm pears such as Bosc or Anjou,
peeled, halved, and cored

3 tablespoons unsalted butter

¼ cup (2 fl oz/60 ml) Grand Marnier
or other orange-flavored liqueur

6 fresh mint sprigs

This dessert is a warm marriage of pears and citrus fruit, highlights of the winter season. If blood oranges, with their dramatic red flesh, are unavailable, substitute any other sweet orange. For an additional flourish, reserve the orange zest in the cooking liquid to use as a garnish.

SERVES 6

❋ In a nonaluminum saucepan over medium heat, combine the sugar and water. Bring to a boil, stirring to dissolve the sugar. Add the cinnamon stick, orange zest, and the juice of 1 of the blood oranges. Reduce the heat to medium-low and add the pear halves. Place a small plate or similar weight in the pan to keep the pears immersed in the poaching liquid. Cook until the pears are tender, 30–45 minutes. Be careful not to overcook. Drain, reserving the liquid, and let the pears cool slightly. Strain the poaching liquid through a fine-mesh sieve into a measuring pitcher. Set aside.

❋ Using a sharp knife, cut a thick slice off the top and bottom of each remaining orange, removing all the white membrane to reveal the flesh. Then, standing each orange upright, cut off the peel and white membrane in thick, wide strips. Thinly slice the oranges crosswise.

❋ In a large sauté pan over medium heat, melt the butter. Add half of the orange slices and cook, stirring gently, until softened, 2–3 minutes. Raise the heat to high. Pour in the Grand Marnier and deglaze the pan, stirring with a wooden spoon to dislodge any bits from the pan bottom. Reduce the heat to medium, add 1½ cups (12 fl oz/375 ml) of the reserved poaching liquid to the oranges, and cook until the liquid is heated through, 3–4 minutes longer.

❋ To serve, divide the cooked oranges and their cooking liquid among shallow individual bowls. Place each pear half, flat side down, on a cutting board and cut lengthwise into thin slices, leaving the slices attached at the narrow end. Arrange a pear half in each bowl, fanning out the slices. Top with the reserved uncooked orange slices. Garnish each bowl with a mint sprig and serve.

NUTRITIONAL ANALYSIS PER SERVING: Calories 479 (Kilojoules 2,012); Protein 1 g; Carbohydrates 105 g; Total Fat 6 g; Saturated Fat 4 g; Cholesterol 16 mg; Sodium 2 mg; Dietary Fiber 5 g

Peach and Toasted Almond Ice Cream

PREP TIME: 20 MINUTES, PLUS
1½ HOURS FOR CHILLING
AND FREEZING

COOKING TIME: 20 MINUTES

INGREDIENTS

½ cup (2½ oz/75 g) slivered blanched
  almonds

1 lb (500 g) ripe peaches, peeled,
  pitted, and coarsely chopped

1 cup (8 oz/240 g) sugar

1 tablespoon lemon juice

2 cups (16 fl oz/500 ml) milk

2 cups (16 fl oz/500 ml) heavy
  (double) cream

1 vanilla bean (pod)

6 egg yolks

ice cubes as needed

PREP TIP: Peel peaches the same way
you would a tomato. See the technique illustrated on page 13.

Peaches tend to be at their most flavorful at the height of summer, the best time to make this delicious ice cream. The ice-
cream base lends itself to mixing with other fruits and nuts as
well, such as pears, raspberries, or pecans.

MAKES 2 QT (2 L); SERVES 8

❀ Preheat an oven to 350°F (180°C). Spread the almonds on a baking
sheet and toast until fragrant and just beginning to color, 5–7 minutes.
Transfer to a dish and let cool.

❀ In a food processor, combine the peaches, ¼ cup (2 oz/60 g) of the
sugar, and the lemon juice and purée until smooth. Set aside.

❀ In a heavy saucepan, combine the milk, cream, and the remaining
¾ cup (6 oz/180 g) sugar. Cut the vanilla bean in half lengthwise and,
using the tip of a knife, scrape the seeds into the milk mixture, then
drop in the bean pods as well. Place over medium heat and, stirring
constantly, heat until small bubbles appear along the edges of the pan.
Remove from the heat and remove and discard the bean pod.

❀ In a bowl, whisk the egg yolks until pale yellow and thickened. Slowly
pour in the hot milk mixture while whisking continuously. Pour the
mixture into the saucepan and place over low heat. Cook, stirring constantly, until the mixture coats the back of a wooden spoon, 5–7 minutes. Remove from the heat and pour through a fine-mesh sieve into a
clean bowl. Nest the bowl in another bowl of ice to cool. When cool, stir
in the peach purée and almonds. Cover and refrigerate for at least 1 hour
or for up to 3 hours.

❀ Transfer the peach mixture to an ice-cream maker and freeze according to the manufacturer's instructions. Serve at once or freeze for up
to 3 days.

NUTRITIONAL ANALYSIS PER SERVING: Calories 469 (Kilojoules 1970); Protein 7 g;
Carbohydrates 40 g; Total Fat 33 g; Saturated Fat 17 g; Cholesterol 250 mg; Sodium 59 mg;
Dietary Fiber 2 g

Coconut Biscotti

PREP TIME: 30 MINUTES

COOKING TIME: 50 MINUTES

INGREDIENTS

2¾ cups (14 oz/440 g) all-purpose (plain) flour

1 teaspoon baking powder

½ teaspoon baking soda (bicarbonate of soda)

½ teaspoon salt

4 eggs

¾ cup (6 oz/185 g) sugar

2 teaspoons vanilla extract (essence)

1 tablespoon grated lemon zest

1 cup (4 oz/125 g) sweetened shredded coconut

SERVING TIP: For an elegant touch, coat one end of each cookie with chocolate: Melt 8 ounces (250 g) chopped semisweet (plain) chocolate in a heatproof bowl set over (but not touching) simmering water, stirring frequently until smooth. Dip one end of each cookie into the chocolate, then place on a baking sheet lined with parchment (baking) paper. Refrigerate until the chocolate sets.

These crisp Italian cookies are a natural match for steaming cups of espresso.

MAKES ABOUT 3 DOZEN BISCOTTI

❋ Preheat an oven to 325°F (165°C). Line 2 baking sheets with parchment (baking) paper.

❋ In a large bowl, stir together the flour, baking powder, baking soda, and salt. In another bowl, beat together the eggs and sugar until well blended and light. Stir in the vanilla, lemon zest, and coconut and mix well. Add the flour mixture and stir just until blended to form a stiff and slightly sticky dough.

❋ Divide the dough in half. Transfer half to each prepared baking sheet and form each into a log 12 inches (30 cm) long and 3 inches (7.5 cm) wide.

❋ Bake until firm, about 30 minutes. Remove from the oven and let cool slightly. Reduce the oven temperature to 275°F (135°C).

❋ Using a serrated knife, cut the logs on the diagonal into slices ½ inch (12 mm) wide. Return the slices, cut sides down, to the parchment-lined baking sheets. Bake until lightly toasted, about 20 minutes. Transfer to racks and let cool completely. Store in an airtight container at room temperature for up to 1 week.

NUTRITIONAL ANALYSIS PER COOKIE: Calories 82 (Kilojoules 344); Protein 2 g; Carbohydrates 15 g; Total Fat 2 g; Saturated Fat 1 g; Cholesterol 24 mg; Sodium 77 mg; Dietary Fiber 1 g

Passion Fruit Sorbet

PREP TIME: 15 MINUTES, PLUS
2½ HOURS FOR CHILLING
AND FREEZING

COOKING TIME: 5 MINUTES

INGREDIENTS

¾ cup (6 oz/185 g) sugar

1¾ cups (14 fl oz/430 ml) plus
2 tablespoons water

9 ripe passion fruits

½ pt (4 oz/125 g) ripe strawberries

PREP TIP: Passion fruits are ready to eat when they look overripe and their leathery purple-brown skins are deeply wrinkled. Smooth-skinned fruits will ripen at room temperature in about 5 days. Store ripe fruit in the refrigerator for several days, or scoop out the pulp and freeze it for up to several months.

Passion fruits, which grow in the subtropics, have a unique, very sweet, floral flavor and aroma. They are at their peak in spring. You can substitute ½ cup (4 fl oz/125 ml) purée of any fruit that is in season. Strawberries make a nice garnish, especially tiny fraises des bois, also in season in the spring.

SERVES 4

❁ In a saucepan over medium heat, combine the sugar and the 1¾ cups (14 fl oz/430 ml) plus 2 tablespoons water. Heat, stirring, until the sugar dissolves and a syrup forms, about 5 minutes. Set aside.

❁ Cut each passion fruit in half and scoop out the seeds and pulp into a sieve placed over a bowl. Using the back of a spoon, push the pulp through the sieve, pressing firmly against the seeds to release as much juice as possible. Set the juice aside. Add the seeds to the sugar syrup, stirring to extract additional flavor from them. Then pour the syrup through the sieve into another bowl. Discard the seeds and let the syrup cool. Stir the passion fruit purée into the syrup. Cover and refrigerate for at least 1 hour or for up to 3 hours.

❁ Transfer the passion fruit base to an ice-cream maker and freeze according to the manufacturer's instructions until slightly firm, about 30 minutes. Transfer to a container with a tight-fitting lid and freeze for at least 1 hour or for up to 3 days.

❁ To serve, spoon into chilled individual glasses and sprinkle the strawberries over the top.

NUTRITIONAL ANALYSIS PER SERVING: Calories 212 (Kilojoules 890); Protein 1 g; Carbohydrates 54 g; Total Fat 0 g; Saturated Fat 0 g; Cholesterol 0 mg; Sodium 12 mg; Dietary Fiber 1 g

Berry Tart with Granola Crust

PREP TIME: 35 MINUTES, PLUS
1 HOUR FOR CHILLING

COOKING TIME: 35 MINUTES,
PLUS 30 MINUTES FOR
COOLING

INGREDIENTS

FOR THE PASTRY

1 cup (5 oz/155 g) all-purpose (plain) flour

1¼ cups (7½ oz/225 g) plain toasted granola

¼ teaspoon salt

½ cup (4 oz/125 g) chilled unsalted butter, cut into tablespoon-sized pieces

4–5 tablespoons (2–3 fl oz/60–80 ml) ice water

FOR THE FILLING

½ cup (4 fl oz/125 ml) heavy (double) cream

½ lb (250 g) cream cheese, at room temperature

⅓ cup (1½ oz/45 g) confectioners' (icing) sugar

4 cups (1 lb/500 g) berries (see note)

What tops this tart depends upon the season. Spring strawberries are wonderful, as are summer's yellow raspberries, mulberries, blackberries, boysenberries, red currants, and blueberries. Combine them in whatever mix suits your taste. Place the berries on the tart at the last minute so the juices do not bleed into the filling.

MAKES ONE 9-INCH (23-CM) TART; SERVES 8

❈ To make the pastry, in a food processor, combine the flour, ½ cup (3 oz/90 g) of the granola, and the salt. Process to mix. With the machine running, drop in the butter pieces, one at a time, and process until evenly distributed. Using on-off pulses, add only as much of the water as needed for the dough to hold together. Do not overprocess, or the dough will be tough. Form into a ball, flatten into a disk, and wrap in plastic wrap. Refrigerate for at least 1 hour or for up to 12 hours.

❈ Preheat an oven to 350°F (180°C).

❈ On a lightly floured work surface, roll out the dough into a round 11 inches (28 cm) in diameter and ¼ inch (6 mm) thick. Drape the pastry over the rolling pin and carefully transfer to a 9-inch (23-cm) tart pan with a removable bottom. Gently ease the pastry into the pan and trim even with the pan rim. Sprinkle ½ cup (3 oz/90 g) of the remaining granola over the bottom and press lightly. Line the pastry with parchment (baking) paper and fill with pastry weights or beans. Bake until firm and lightly colored, about 35 minutes. Remove from the oven and remove the weights and parchment. Let cool completely on a rack.

❈ To make the filling, pour the cream into a bowl. Using a whisk or an electric mixer, beat until soft peaks form. In another bowl, combine the cream cheese and confectioners' sugar and beat until smooth. Using a rubber spatula, fold the whipped cream into the cream cheese mixture.

❈ Spread the cheese mixture in the bottom of the tart shell. Arrange the berries over the top and sprinkle with the remaining ¼ cup (1½ oz/45 g) granola. Cut into wedges and serve.

NUTRITIONAL ANALYSIS PER SERVING: Calories 491 (Kilojoules 2,062); Protein 8 g; Carbohydrates 43 g; Total Fat 32 g; Saturated Fat 20 g; Cholesterol 83 mg; Sodium 172 mg; Dietary Fiber 4 g

Cranberry Crème Brûlée

PREP TIME: 20 MINUTES, PLUS
2 HOURS FOR CHILLING

COOKING TIME: 45 MINUTES

INGREDIENTS

2 cups (8 oz/250 g) cranberries, halved

½ cup (4 oz/120 g) granulated sugar

3 cups (24 fl oz/750 ml) heavy (double) cream

1 piece vanilla bean (pod), 2 inches (5 cm) long

8 egg yolks

½ cup (3½ oz/105 g) firmly packed brown sugar

COOKING TIP: A quick and easy way to caramelize the sugar is to use a small propane torch. Move the flame back and forth across the top, watching carefully so the sugar does not burn.

Cranberries provide a tart surprise in this creamy autumn dessert. In other seasons, substitute your favorite fruit—try fresh berries or diced peaches—adjusting the amount of sugar to the sweetness of the fruit. See the tip on page 95 regarding cooking in a hot-water bath.

SERVES 8

❋ Preheat an oven to 350°F (180°C). Lightly butter the bottom of eight ½-cup (4–fl oz/125-ml) ramekins.

❋ In a bowl, toss the cranberries with ¼ cup (2 oz/60 g) of the granulated sugar. Divide evenly among the prepared ramekins.

❋ Pour the cream into a heavy saucepan. Cut the vanilla bean in half lengthwise and, using the tip of a knife, scrape the seeds into the cream. Drop in the bean pods as well. Place over medium heat and stir constantly until small bubbles appear along the edges of the pan; set aside.

❋ In a bowl, whisk together the egg yolks and the remaining ¼ cup (2 oz/60 g) granulated sugar until pale yellow and thickened.

❋ Remove the bean pods from the cream. Slowly drizzle the hot cream into the egg yolks while whisking continuously. Then pour the mixture into the saucepan. Place the saucepan over low heat and cook, stirring constantly, until the mixture coats the back of a wooden spoon, 7–10 minutes. Remove from the heat and pour through a fine-mesh sieve into the prepared ramekins, dividing evenly. Place the ramekins in a large baking dish and pour hot water into the dish to reach halfway up the sides of the ramekins.

❋ Bake until set and a knife inserted into the center comes out clean, 20–25 minutes. Transfer to a rack and let cool completely. Cover and refrigerate for at least 2 hours or for up to 12 hours.

❋ Just before serving, preheat a broiler (griller). Sprinkle the brown sugar evenly over the tops of the ramekins. Place under the broiler about 3 inches (7.5 cm) from the heat source and broil (grill) until the sugar caramelizes, about 2 minutes. Watch carefully so the sugar doesn't burn. Remove from the broiler and serve immediately.

NUTRITIONAL ANALYSIS PER SERVING: Calories 493 (Kilojoules 2,071); Protein 5 g; Carbohydrates 33 g; Total Fat 39 g; Saturated Fat 23 g; Cholesterol 338 mg; Sodium 56 mg; Dietary Fiber 1 g

GLOSSARY

BEANS

From early spring through autumn, markets offer many kinds of fresh beans. Dried beans are available year-round.

CHICKPEAS

Also known as garbanzos, these resemble large, tan peas and have a rich, nut-like flavor.

FAVA BEANS

Also known as broad beans, these wonderfully sweet and tender beans are available fresh from early spring to early summer. (To prepare fava beans, see the instructions on page 12.)

FLAGEOLETS

Small, pale green beans encased in slender green pods, fresh flageolets are in season from midsummer through autumn. The bulk of the crop, however, is dried to serve as a pantry staple.

HARICOTS VERTS

Slender, delicate French variety of green beans, also known as fillet beans. Available in summer.

WHITE BEANS

Popular varieties include navy, Boston, and Great Northern, noted for their mild flavor and smooth, creamy texture.

YELLOW WAX

Variety of fresh beans distinguished by pale, waxy yellow pod.

BROCCOLI, CHINESE

This member of the cabbage family has small, sprouting heads and long stems with tender leaves. Chinese broccoli, which is usually cut up and steamed or stir-fried, may be found in Asian stores or farmers' markets.

BROCCOLI RABE

This pleasantly bitter, strong-flavored green is available from autumn to spring.

CELERY ROOT

Also known as celeriac or celery knob, this variety of celery is grown specifically for its root. The thick skin is peeled away to reveal a crisp, ivory flesh with a sweet celery flavor. The flesh should be dipped in a mixture of water and lemon juice to prevent discoloration.

CHEESES

As well as providing protein and calcium, cheese adds variety and rich taste to a vegetarian diet. Because cheese is often high in fat and sodium, it should be used judiciously.

CAMEMBERT

A rich, creamy French cow's milk cheese formed into small, plump wheels and covered with a dusty, white edible rind.

CHEDDAR

A semifirm cheese that ranges in taste from mild and mellow when fairly young to sharp and tangy when aged for 9 months or longer.

GOAT CHEESE

Although many different kinds of cheese are made from goat's milk, the most common ones are fresh and creamy and have a sharp, tangy flavor. They are sometimes coated with pepper, ash, or mixtures of herbs.

GORGONZOLA

This Italian blue-veined cheese, originating in the town of Gorgonzola near Milan, is prized for its creamy texture and strong, sharp, almost spicy flavor.

MOZZARELLA

A rindless white Italian cheese with a mild flavor and soft texture. Mozzarella is traditionally made from water buffalo's milk and sold fresh, floating in water. More widely available is fresh mozzarella made from cow's milk, sold in water or packaged.

PARMESAN

Aged for at least 2 years until it has a firm texture, a thick crust, and a full, sharp, salty flavor, this cow's milk cheese is used as a seasoning, grated over pasta, or added to stuffings or fillings. Buy Parmesan in block form and grate it fresh as needed. The finest Italian variety is designated Parmigiano-Reggiano®.

RICOTTA

This light-textured, mild-tasting Italian cheese is naturally lower in fat than many cheeses, and even more so when made from part-skim milk.

CHILES

Ranging from mild to fiery hot, chiles add fire and flavor to a range of dishes. When handling any chile, observe basic precautions that prevent painful burning caused by their volatile oils (see page 13).

ANAHEIM

A large, slender green chile (below) that can be mild or slightly hot. Also called California chile.

JALAPEÑO

A fiery chile distinguished by its thick flesh and small, tapered body (below, top) measuring about 2½ inches (6 cm) long and 1½ inches (4 cm) wide. Dried, smoked jalapeños, called chipotles, are often sold canned in a thick, vinegary adobo sauce.

SERRANO

This tiny chile (above, bottom) is as hot as a jalapeño but has a distinctly sharper taste.

CHILE PASTE

A popular Asian seasoning made with hot red chiles, salt, usually vinegar, and often garlic. Just a touch of the paste adds a rich, fiery taste.

COCONUT MILK

Not the water inside the nut, but a creamy liquid extracted from grated coconut meat. Look for canned coconut milk in Indian, Asian, or Caribbean markets and well-stocked food stores. Before using, shake to reincorporate the cream that rises to the top. Or, to reduce the fat, spoon off the cream and use the lighter liquid beneath it.

CORN, BABY

These tiny ears of immature corn are so tender that the entire ear, including the cob, can be eaten. Fresh ears of baby corn 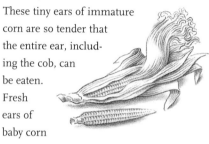 are occasionally seen in farmers' markets. More often you'll find them canned in Asian markets.

EGGPLANTS

Appreciated for its rich taste and texture, eggplant stars in many vegetarian dishes. Also known as aubergine, it's available year-round, though it is at its peak in summer. The skins of these vegetable fruits vary in color from purple to red and from yellow to white, and their shapes range from small and oval to long and slender to large and pear shaped. Slender, purple Asian eggplants have a milder flavor and fewer seeds than the larger varieties.

GINGER

This sweet-hot seasoning is the underground stem, or rhizome, of the tropical ginger plant. Delicately flavored young ginger, with its fragile skin and pink tips, is found in Asian stores, specialty greengrocers, and farmers' markets in spring; more mature ginger is available year-round.

GREEN GARLIC

Immature heads of garlic picked before the cloves are defined, with a sweet, mild flavor.

JERUSALEM ARTICHOKES

These tuberous vegetables, which look like small potatoes, get their name in part because their flavor resembles an artichoke. Available year-round but at their best in winter.

JICAMA

The thick, brown peel of this root conceals a crisp, slightly sweet flesh that is eaten raw. Available year-round, it is at its peak from winter to midspring.

LEAF VEGETABLES

Many kinds of leaf vegetables, both raw and cooked, grace the vegetarian table. Their varied colors, tastes, and textures offer cooks tremendous variety.

ESCAROLE

Also known as Batavian endive, this member of the chicory family has broad, green, loose leaves with a refreshingly bitter flavor.

KALE

At peak of season from late autumn through winter, this member of the mustard family has a strong, spicy taste and robust texture that are best enjoyed cooked.

HERBS

Herbs are used to flavor many vegetarian dishes. Refrigerate fresh herbs, either with their stems in a glass of water or wrapped in damp paper towels inside a plastic bag.

BASIL

This sweet, spicy, tender-leafed herb goes especially well with tomatoes. Special basil varieties are found in well-stocked food stores and farmers' markets, including purple-leafed opal basil, which has a more pronounced flavor.

CHERVIL

A springtime herb with small leaves and a taste reminiscent of parsley and anise. Use fresh in salads and with carrots.

CILANTRO

Also called fresh coriander and Chinese parsley, this herb has flat, frilly leaves, which resemble flat-leaf (Italian) parsley. Its highly aromatic taste complements the cooking of India, China, Southeast Asia, and Mexico.

GARLIC CHIVES

Known for their mild garlic flavor, garlic chives have flat, broad leaves and large white blossoms. Use fresh in salads and in dishes featuring eggs or cheese. The best way to cut any variety of chives is to snip them with kitchen scissors.

MARJORAM

This Mediterranean herb has a milder flavor than its close relative, oregano. Pair it with tomatoes, eggplants, and bean dishes.

PARSLEY, FLAT-LEAF

Also called Italian parsley, this herb has a stronger flavor than the curly variety.

TARRAGON

With its distinctively sweet flavor reminiscent of anise, tarragon is used to flavor salad dressings, eggs, and vegetables.

THYME

A fragrant, clean-tasting, small-leaved herb from the eastern Mediterranean, popular fresh or dried.

MÂCHE

Also known as lamb's lettuce or corn salad, this early spring salad green (below) has delicate flavor and texture.

OAKLEAF LETTUCE

This loose-leafed lettuce has large, tender, mild leaves with rusty-red fringes.

RADICCHIO

This crisp, red-and-white leafed chicory grows in small round or elongated heads and has a refreshingly bitter taste.

SWISS CHARD

Similar to spinach although somewhat milder, Swiss chard has dark green leaves and crisp white or red stems. Also known as chard or silverbeet.

LEEKS

At their best from early spring through autumn, leeks are sweet and mild when cooked. The tender white parts have a delicate flavor and are often used alone; the tougher greens, however, may be included in long-cooked dishes. Grown in sandy soil, leeks

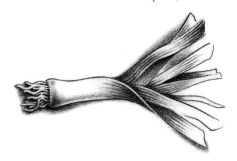

should be rinsed thoroughly with cold running water to remove any grit lodged between their leaves. Slit them lengthwise to make cleaning easier.

LEMONGRASS

This tropical grass has a bright, lemonlike flavor. Look for it in well-stocked food stores, Southeast Asian markets, and some farmers' markets.

MASA HARINA

Finely ground lime-slaked corn, masa harina is available in well-stocked food stores and Mexican markets. It's traditionally used to make tortilla and tamale doughs.

NOODLES

Noodles are part of many satisfying vegetarian main courses and are rich in protein and complex carbohydrates.

BEAN THREADS

Dried threadlike noodles made from mung beans. When soaked, they become transparent, leading to such alternative names as cellophane noodles and glass noodles. Available in Asian markets and some food stores.

CAPELLINI

"Little hairs" in Italian, this term describes fine strands of dried semolina pasta.

RICE STICKS

Made from rice flour, these dried noodles come in a variety of thicknesses. Sold in Asian markets and well-stocked food stores.

SOBA

Thin Japanese noodles made from buckwheat flour alone or a mixture of buckwheat and whole-wheat flours. They have a satisfyingly earthy texture and taste, distinguished by a slightly sour tang.

MUSHROOMS

With their earthy flavor and meaty texture, mushrooms add substance to many vegetarian dishes.

OYSTER

This tender Asian variety is named for its pale grayish color, shellfishlike shape, and faint resemblance in taste to oysters.

PORCINI

Prized for their meaty texture and rich flavor, porcini are found fresh in autumn. Dried porcini are sold in Italian delicatessens and specialty-food stores. Also known as cèpes.

PORTOBELLO

The flat brown caps of these mushrooms grow up to 4 inches (10 cm) or more in diameter. They are enjoyed for their rich taste and texture.

SHIITAKE

These are prized for their rich flavor and chewy texture, whether fresh or dried and reconstituted in warm water. Their flat circular caps have a distinctive velvety dark brown color. Trim the tough stems before cooking.

STRAW

Small, plump brown mushrooms resembling closed umbrellas, named after the beds of straw on which they are cultivated. Most commonly found canned in Asian food stores.

WHITE

These mild-tasting mushrooms have white caps and short stems. Immature white mushrooms with caps that have not yet opened are sometimes called button mushrooms.

PARSNIPS

Available autumn through spring, but best after winter's cold has converted their starch to sugar, parsnips have a shape, size, and texture similar to carrots. When cooked, they have a sweet, almost nutlike taste.

SEMOLINA FLOUR

Coarse-textured flour ground from hard durum wheat. In Italy, semolina flour is preferred for making both dried and fresh pastas.

SHALLOTS

Brown-skinned, purple-tinged cousins of onions and garlic, shallots have a flavor resembling a cross between their kin.

SPICES

Buy spices in small quantities, as their flavor tends to diminish rapidly. Store in airtight containers away from heat and light. For the best flavor, buy whole spices and grind them in an electric spice mill or a mortar as needed.

CARAWAY SEEDS

Mildly spicy caraway seeds go especially well with breads and such robust vegetables as potatoes, cabbage, carrots, and mushrooms.

CARDAMOM

A sweet spice favored in India and the Middle East, particularly in rice dishes, pickles, and curries; and in Scandinavian, German, and Russian baked goods. The small, round seeds are enclosed inside a pod that is easily split open to remove them for grinding.

CORIANDER

The small, spicy-sweet seeds of the coriander plant, and the source of fresh cilantro or Chinese parsley. Use whole or ground.

CUMIN

Small, crescent-shaped seeds favored in Indian, Middle Eastern, and Mexican cooking. Their dusky aroma goes well with vegetables.

CURRY POWDER

A spice blend used to flavor curries. Common ingredients are coriander, cumin, ground dried chile, fenugreek, and turmeric.

GARAM MASALA

A spice blend of northern India that usually includes cumin, coriander, cardamom, cloves, cinnamon, and pepper. Available in Indian markets and well-stocked food stores. To make your own, see page 31.

TURMERIC

This powdered spice imparts a bright yellow color and a mildly pungent, earthy taste to dishes to which it has been added.

SQUASHES, WINTER

Harvested in the fall, hard-shelled winter squashes of many kinds bring color and rich taste and texture to vegetarian menus.

BUTTERNUT

Appreciated for its bright orange, sweet flesh, the butternut squash is cylindrical and up to

12 inches (30 cm) long, with its flower end slightly enlarged in a distinctive bulb-like shape.

HUBBARD

This squash's relatively unattractive, greenish gray shell and large, irregular shape conceals flavorful, rich orange flesh.

SPAGHETTI

An elongated, yellow-skinned squash with flesh that separates into mild, spaghettilike strands when cooked.

TABLE QUEEN

Also known as golden acorn squash for its orange flesh and acornlike shape. Its golden meat has a mild, sweet flavor.

TOMATILLOS

The loose, brown, papery husks of fresh tomatillos are easily torn away to reveal the small, shiny-skinned green fruits inside. Tomatillos contribute a tart, astringent flavor to fresh and cooked sauces, particularly in Mexican cooking. Most well-stocked food stores also carry canned tomatillos.

TOMATOES

In season, many kinds of tomatoes may be found in greengrocers and farmers' markets.

CHERRY

Cherry-sized tomatoes, either red or yellow, with sweet, juicy flesh.

GREEN

Underripe tomatoes, prized for their tang and their crisp texture.

PLUM

Roughly the size and shape of an egg, this Italian variety, also known as Roma tomato, offers reliable flavor and texture year-round, even when good sun-ripened summer tomatoes are unavailable.

YELLOW PEAR

Small tomatoes with bright yellow skin and flesh. Also called teardrop tomatoes.

ZEST

The outermost, brightly colored layer of a citrus fruit's rind, rich in flavorful oils. Citrus zest may be removed with a fine grater; with a swivel-bladed vegetable peeler or a special citrus "stripper"; or with the small, sharp-edged holes of a citrus "zester." Always take care not to remove any of the bitter white pith beneath the zest.

INDEX

ACKNOWLEDGMENTS

The publishers would like to thank the following people and associations for their generous assistance and support in producing this book: Desne Border, Ken DellaPenta, Jennifer Hanson, Hill Nutrition Associates, Sharilyn Hovind, Lisa Lee, and Cecily Upton.

The following kindly lent props for photography: Fillamento, Williams-Sonoma, and Pottery Barn, San Francisco, CA. The contributions of the staff at Real Foods of San Francisco, CA, were greatly appreciated. The photographer would also like to thank Mike and Joan Mortensson for generously sharing their lovely farm with us for our location setting. Foxglove Farm is located in Sebastopol, CA. Additionally, we would like to thank Chromeworks and ProCamera, San Francisco, CA, and FUJI Film. Special acknowledgment goes to Daniel Yearwood for the beautiful backgrounds and surface treatments.